*P*resented to

_____

by _____

date _____

"May the Lord bless you and keep you;
the Lord make his face to shine upon you,
and be gracious to you;
the Lord lift up his countenance upon you,
and give you peace."

Numbers 6.24-26

Blessings

AND

Prayers

FOR HOME AND FAMILY

Canadian Conference of Catholic Bishops
Ottawa Canada

Blessings and Prayers for Home and Family
U.S. Edition
National Liturgy Office
Canadian Conference of Catholic Bishops

Original art and design by CCCB Publications
Cover design by Tom A. Wright

The English translation of *Magnificat, Benedictus, Nunc dimittis, Doxology* and *Lord's Prayer* by
   International Consultation on English Texts (ICET).

Litany of Loreto, see: *Suppliche litaniche a santa Maria* – Mariale Servorum 5 (Curia generalis
   OSM, Romae 1988), pages 321-324; Biblical Litany to Saint Mary, pages 325-327; Litany of
   Saint Mary of Hope, pages 328-330.

Litany to St. Joseph: This Litany is an adapted English translation from the draft of an
   Italian Servite booklet *In onore di san Giuseppe, sposo della beata Vergine Maria,
   compatrono dell'Ordine*, pages 334-335.

Published by ACTA Publications, 5559 W. Howard Street, Skokie, IL 60077-2621.
   (800) 397-2282, www.actapublications.com.

ISBN: 978-0-87946-380-9

LCN: 2008931392

Printed in the United States of America by Evangel Press.

Year 15 14 13 12 11 10 09 08

Printing 15 14 13 12 11 10 9 8 7 6 5 4 3 2 First

CONTENTS

CONTENTS (Continued)

CONTENTS (Continued)

CONTENTS (Continued)

PREFACE

This beautiful book of blessings and prayers for home and family use was originally published by the Canadian Conference of Catholic Bishops. ACTA Publications is pleased to offer this U.S. edition. Here is the Preface by the Most Reverend Gerald Wiesner, O.M.I., Bishop of Prince George, the Chairman of the Episcopal Commission for Liturgy:

God's people are exhorted to bless the Lord at all times and to pray unceasingly as we await the Lord's return in glory. While the Church fulfills this uniquely in the celebration of the Eucharist, each Christian and especially each family of Christians must take this responsibility to heart.

On great occasions and in simple moments of personal joy or pain, we turn to the God who is always close to us and acknowledge his saving and supporting presence. Many of these moments take place at home, but that does not mean that they are beyond the ministry of the Church. In these moments, it is the family itself that becomes the Church in miniature, the domestic Church, as it celebrates the important moments in life. Leading the family in prayer should be one of the great joys of parents.

Marking important family moments with celebration and prayer, especially when children are young, teaches and encourages habits that will move from family to family as they become virtual family traditions. These occasions will also provide individuals with the tools of personal prayer, moments to mark situations in our lives and in the events around us.

The prayers and prayer services presented here are meant to both teach and sustain families in celebrating the important moments in life, times of joy and sorrow. Although these moments do not occur within the church building, they are moments in the life of the entire Church, times when we celebrate our membership in the holy People of God.

+ *Gerald Wiesner, omi*

Most Reverend Gerald Wiesner, O.M.I.
Bishop of Prince George
Chairman, Episcopal Commission for Liturgy
Canadian Conference of Catholic Bishops

INTRODUCTION

This book is intended primarily for use in families or small communities. It provides a reference for families or small faith groups – cornerstones of the parish community – to live the mission of Christ that flows from the Sunday Eucharist and to build up the Body of Christ. Family and community life provide many opportunities to praise and bless God and to intercede for the needs of the Church, world, community, and those in need.

Rejoicing at baptism, confirmation, first communion or marriage; celebrating a birthday, anniversary or graduation; gathering around a sick member; people of faith turn to God to rejoice in the many events that mark our physical and spiritual growth and to seek consolation in God's healing presence.

To bless and praise God is the fundamental response of the Christian to God's mighty works. To bless God is to remember, recall, and invoke God's presence and assistance, as well as to offer our praise.

CELEBRATING BLESSINGS

Jesus passed on to us the Jewish tradition of blessing. In many tender scenes in the gospels, Jesus touches and blesses. He welcomes little children, puts his arms around them, and blesses them (Mark 10.13-16). When at table, Jesus blesses food (Mark 6.41). As he ascends into heaven, he raises his hands and blesses the disciples (Luke 24.50-51).

MEANING

The word "blessing" has two distinct and related meanings: It refers to our praise of God and to our request for his loving care for us (see Psalms 134 and 115). As we praise God over people and things, they are blessed for his service.

Blessings and Prayers for Home and Family

When Celebrated

A blessing may be celebrated at any appropriate time.

* In the course of the day: We probably do not realize how blessings are a part of our daily routine. In the Jewish tradition, a blessing or prayer is associated with each activity of life: awaking, rising, and beginning any action, such as eating, working, or praying. Christians continue this tradition as we dedicate the new day to the glory of God and pray that our work may enrich others as it enriches our lives. We bless God for the food we eat; we praise and ask him to bless the work we do.

* During the week and year: This daily tradition is continued when the Christian family gathers to worship God on the Lord's Day and other occasions, such as the celebration of sacraments. In baptism, the water is blessed before the candidates are plunged into it; in marriage, the rings may be blessed before the bride and groom give them to each other.

* Special Occasions: A community or a family may celebrate other blessings whenever these are fitting in their lives. Scripture and prayer may surround the blessing.

Blessings put us in touch with four realities of the Christian life: creation, revelation, salvation, and mission.

* Creation: Blessings remind us that we are merely stewards of God's creation. Everything belongs to God, and we will have to give an account of our use of this precious gift. Blessings remind us that creation is good, that it is both gift and sacred trust.

* Revelation: Blessings flow from the fact that God has revealed himself to us and called us to be his own. We could not fully know God as we do if he had not revealed his presence and his law to us. To bless God is to acknowledge with gratitude this self-revealing God who created us and called us.

* Salvation: Blessings acknowledge that God the Creator is also the God who sent his Son into the world. Jesus Christ not only reveals the mercy and love of God, but also gives his life to save us from the evil we injected into God's creation. We turned away from God, the giver of life. In Christ, God has found us and welcomed us back. In gratitude we bless God. Salvation is accomplished by the

mystery of the incarnation of Jesus, the Word-made-flesh. This is an affirmation of the goodness of creation. The Creator becomes part of his creation. Jesus is born in human history of a woman and takes on our flesh and blood. Now Christ uses the elements of creation to become signs of and means to salvation. This means that God touches us through the material world and communicates his divine love and life through sacramental signs, which are created things.

- Mission: Not only did God love the world so much that he gave us his only Son to save us, but God also renews that call in the new covenant of the Cross. As God shares his creating power with us in the gift of creation, so Christ shares his mission of salvation with the Church, his body. We are commissioned to bring the good news of salvation to all people. The Christian task is the total transformation of the world: to restore all things in Christ, so that he may hand over the redeemed kingdom to his Father. By using creation in a right way, we both sanctify it and are sanctified by God's gifts. We also seek to live and use it in conformity with God's will.

LITURGY AND FAMILY LIFE

We tend to think of blessings and liturgical ceremonies as those celebrated in a church. But in a broader sense, liturgy is also celebrated in our homes and families. In a family or community that seeks to grow in Christ, home liturgies build on the strengths and values of the parish community and lead to a deepening of the life in the Spirit of the Lord Jesus. A family or community, striving to be Christ-like, can be centered on the Eucharist. All aspects of its life and prayer lead up to the Sunday celebration and are nourished by it. The prayer life of individuals and families prepares them for Mass, and helps them to live the Mass throughout the week. The living sacrifice that they offer with Christ is not restricted to Sunday, but is part of their daily carrying of the Cross.

Catholic Book of Worship (CBW) provides music for many psalms and hymns for these celebrations. The extensive pastoral notes and liturgical index of the choir edition of *CBW II* and *CBW III* provide a key to these musical resources. (Available at www.cccbpublications.ca.)

Ritual Notes

We are creatures of habit. Although we enjoy a change from time to time, most people feel most comfortable when they know what to expect. This is especially true when we live and co-exist with others. Routines help to harmonize relations among people. The same is true of the liturgy in the parish church or in our families and small communities. A regular pattern to prayer helps the family to worship better. Familiar responses, repeated gestures, unified postures and common prayers help us to own the liturgy and, even better, to experience it without being aware of its presence.

Liturgy does not exist for itself but to connect God with us and us with God. Liturgy is like the air or a habit; we need it, but we need not be conscious of its presence. Liturgy, prayer services, and blessings are meant to follow a familiar pattern so all may fully participate in them and encounter the living God. Attention to the ritual elements will help family liturgies to become prayerful. They may be awkward at first, but with use, they become a means to prayer and not an end.

Adapting Texts

The models in this book are of necessity rather general. Those preparing and celebrating blessings should adapt them according to local needs and circumstances: changing from singular to plural; revising words and phrases; adding more scriptural echoes to the prayer of blessing; selecting other readings, psalms, and hymns; choosing other elements or arrangements.

Continuing Influence

Certain blessings and prayers may be attached to specific family celebrations, such as wedding anniversaries, baptismal days, birthdays, and the anniversaries of deceased family members.

The effects of a blessing do not end on the day it is celebrated. Most blessing prayers ask for God's continuing blessing; we know he is always with us in his loving providence. Still, human as we are, we need to have occasions that stir up in us the grace of God, that recall for us the blessings God has given us in the past and those he wants to share with us now.

PASTORAL NOTES

How to Use this Book

The prayers and services in this book are designed primarily for family gatherings. This does not mean that they cannot be used in other situations. Adaptation and flexibility were considerations throughout the assembly of the book. Thus prayers may be shortened by leaving out some sentences or lengthened by the addition of other ideas. Longer scripture readings may be chosen from the list provided or from the Bible or Lectionary. A reflection may be made by the leader or others present and further intentions added to the litanies. The Lord's Prayer may always be included.

A scripture reading and the prayer of blessing (praise) are essential elements. Where no reading is provided in place, the readings from the Mass of the day or the current Sunday are appropriate. In more formal settings, an introduction and final blessing may be added. Gestures may be included such as sprinkling with holy water.

Participation

Although the situation may require that one person lead all the prayers, it is important to involve others present in the celebration. Thus a "reader" is indicated to proclaim the Scripture and announce the intentions. The short intentions and litanies will also be a way of involving others, even young children; they may read the texts provided or add their own. These tasks may be shared with a number of individuals. Songs and acclamations (even the refrain to a well-known hymn) may be included.

Blessings and Prayers for Home and Family

Setting

Some of the services indicated for family may be appropriate in other gatherings. The section on baptism (page 61) may become the opening prayer at a preparation session; this is also true for the prayers around confirmation (page 73). The celebration of engagement may be adapted for a marriage preparation session or for before a wedding rehearsal.

Teachers and students may find the sections on confirmation and first Eucharist helpful as prayers for the classroom, especially with candidates for these sacraments. The Advent wreath and Christmas crib prayers are appropriate during the respective liturgical seasons. Although given as "meal" prayers, the various prayers are appropriate for any gatherings throughout the season, and should be used and adapted as necessary. For example, the Lenten meal prayers (page 250) can be joined with one of the daily Mass readings and used as a morning (daily) prayer for the day; while the service on page 191 is suitable on November 2 (All Souls) or Veterans Day, especially with the prayers on page 108.

Liturgy

Although this book of blessings is primarily for home and family use, some of the prayers may be a useful resource in liturgical settings, including Eucharist.

Blessings usually take place after the homily, ideally as part of the prayer of the faithful; some of the petitions should make reference to the celebration with the blessing prayer used as the closing prayer of the intercessions. Such would be the case for a spring Blessing of Seeds (see page 124) or of Pets (page 129) in conjunction with the feast of St. Francis of Assisi, October 4. Some of the intercessions and the prayer from the Blessing of Families would be appropriate on the feast of the Holy Family (Sunday after Christmas).

The prayers may also be incorporated into the final blessing at Mass or other gatherings. Examples would be Mother's and Father's Day (page 103-104). Thus, during the concluding rite the presider after the greeting (and invitation) offers the prayer and then blesses the assembly.

CREATIVITY

Preparation and care are important aspects of these services; they combine with creativity to bring those involved to a sense of the full, conscious, and active participation at the heart of celebration. Careful preparation and solid effort support these expressions of faith and prayer.

This book provides a resource that encourages and supports the celebration of the important events in the life of God's holy people: within the tradition of the prayer of the Church and proclaiming the wonderful works of God.

Blessing God in Engagement and Marriage

CELEBRATION OF ENGAGEMENT

There may be an informal celebration to praise God and to ask his help when a couple becomes engaged. The two families and close friends may wish to mark the occasion by prayer and celebration. These prayers may be used at a family meal (see pages 8-16) or, if the couple so desires, in a more formal gathering in the home of a family member.

ENGAGEMENT AT HOME

When both families have gathered in a suitable place in the home, the celebration may begin.

INTRODUCTION

The leader begins the prayer service with the sign of the cross and greeting or with a greeting and an invitation to prayer.

Leader: Blessed be the God of love,
who has shown us such great mercy
through his Son, Jesus Christ.
Blessed be God for ever.

All: Blessed be God for ever.

OPENING PRAYER

Leader: Let us pray.

All pause for a moment of silent prayer.

Leader: Lord God, creator of heaven and earth,
in many and varied ways
you have revealed yourself throughout human history,
and now you make yourself known
in the love of *N.* and *N.*.
Grant that we may treasure
your presence in their love
and with them rejoice in your many gifts.

May their faithfulness become an image to all people
of your unending covenant with us.

We ask this through Jesus Christ our Lord.

All: Amen.

Or:

Leader: Lord God,
your love is greater than the human heart,
and your presence is beyond our comprehension.
Look with love upon *N.* and *N.*,
who celebrate their engagement to each other.
Grant that your love may deepen their commitment,
and their love be a sign of your presence in the world.

We ask this through Jesus Christ our Lord.

All: Amen.

SCRIPTURE READING

A brief reading is proclaimed from Scripture.
One of the following texts may be chosen.
The reading may begin in these or similar words.

Leader: Let us listen to these words from Scripture.

Reader: May the God of peace,
who brought back from the dead our Lord Jesus,
the great shepherd of the sheep,
by the blood of the eternal covenant,
make you complete in everything good
so that you may do his will,
working among us
that which is pleasing in his sight,
through Jesus Christ,
to whom be glory forever and ever. Amen.

Hebrews 13.20-21

Or:

Reader: Jesus said:
"You are the salt of the earth;
but if salt has lost its taste,
how can its saltiness be restored?
It is no longer good for anything,
but is thrown out and trampled under foot.
You are the light of the world.
A city built on a hill cannot be hid.
No one after lighting a lamp
puts it under the bushel basket,
but on the lampstand,
and it gives light to all in the house.
In the same way, let your light shine before others,
so that they may see your good works
and give glory to your Father in heaven."

Matthew 5.13-16

Or:

Other Passages:

Also see pages 26-27.

Reflection

The leader or another person may offer a short reflection in which others, especially the couple, may also share.

Litany – Intercessions

A moment of prayer follows. The leader may use the following form, unless the couple would prefer some special prayers (see pages 12-16).

Leader: My brothers and sisters,
let us pray for N. and N.
as we rejoice with them on this happy occasion.

All: R. Lord, hear our prayer.

Another person may read the intentions.

Reader: That God's great love
revealed in Christ Jesus and the Holy Spirit
may deepen in their hearts
with the passing of each day, we pray. R.

That their relationship with each other
may open for them the mystery of God's love, we pray. R.

➤

That they may enjoy the support
of their families and friends
every step of their journey, we pray. *R.*

That they may find in the community of the Church
signs of unity and self-giving love, we pray. *R.*

That their love may bring renewal and joy to all
married couples, we pray. *R.*

That with us
their hearts may become more responsive
to the needs of the world around us, we pray. *R.*

That their preparation
may lead them to a joyful celebration
of their love in (the sacrament of) marriage, we pray. *R.*

PRAYER OF PRAISE

Leader: Blessed are you, Lord God of all creation,
you have created us, male and female, in your image
and bound yourself to your people
in an unbreakable covenant of love.
Loving God, source of all joy,
hear our prayers for *N.* and *N.*,
and grant that the seed of their engagement
may blossom in enduring love and tenderness
in a life of mutual affection and holiness.
We bless you, God, for hearts that seek fulfillment,
for friends that support us,
and for love that reflects your presence to the world.

Glory and praise to you, loving God,
through Jesus Christ our Lord.

All: Amen.

For alternative prayers, see pages 14-16.

If an engagement ring is to be given at this time, the leader may say:

Leader: Glory and honor and praise are yours, O God,
for you have blessed us as your people,
and have called us to serve you in love.
Listen to our prayers for N. and N.,
and bless them
as they prepare for marriage in the Lord.
Grant that this ring
may be a sign of the depths of their love
and a pledge of their fidelity.

All praise to you, almighty and ever-living God,
through Jesus Christ our Lord.

All: Amen.

The ring is given in silence. Then, all may express their support with applause
or another appropriate gesture.

CONCLUSION

Leader: May almighty God bless you.

May God grant you love and happiness,
peace and joy and strength,
all the days of your life.

May God be gracious to all of us,
and pour out his blessings on us,
now and for ever.

All: Amen.

All may exchange a sign of peace.

Engagement at a Family Meal

Before the meal is served and when everyone has taken their place at the table, the celebration may begin.

Invitation to Prayer

The prayer leader begins with the sign of the cross and extends an invitation to spend a moment in quiet prayer.

Leader: Let us bless the Lord,
by whose goodness we live
and by whose grace we love one another.

Or:

Leader: We come together in joy this day
to celebrate the love of N. and N..
Let us bless the Lord.

Scripture Reading

One of those present reads a text from Scripture. One of the following may be used.

The reading may begin in these or similar words.

Leader: Let us listen to these words from Scripture.

Reader: I beg you to lead a life worthy of the calling
to which you have been called,
with all humility and gentleness,
with patience, bearing with one another in love,
making every effort to maintain
the unity of the Spirit in the bond of peace.

cf. *Ephesians* 4.1-3

Or:

Reader: May the Lord make you increase
and abound in love for one another and for all,
just as we abound in love for you.
And may he so strengthen your hearts in holiness
that you may be blameless before our God and Father
at the coming of our Lord Jesus with all his saints.

1 Thessalonians 3.12-13

Or:

Reader: Agree with one another, live in peace,
and the God of love and peace will be with you.

2 Corinthians 13.11b

For other passages, see pages 12-15.

REFLECTION

The leader or another person may offer a short reflection in which others, especially the couple, may also share.

PRAYER FOR THE COUPLE

The leader invites all to pray in silence for a short while and then says one of the following. All may extend one or both hands over or toward the couple.

Leader: Loving God,
our life is in your hands
and so we need not be anxious for the future.

We ask you to bless N. and N..
Send them your light
that they may recognize your will for them.
Direct their steps on the path of life together.

Under your protecting hand
may they spend these days of preparation
in reverent love and responsibility.

With faith in you and in each other
may they grow ever closer together.

We ask this through Jesus Christ our Lord.

All: Amen.

Or:

Leader: Loving God,
source of all joy,
you have created us, male and female, in your image
and betrothed us to yourself
giving us hearts to seek and to serve you
in a shared life of holiness.

You have drawn together *N.* and *N.* in mutual affection
and stirred up in their hearts the desire to marry,
so that, delighting in each other,
they praise you and give you thanks.

May their attraction to each other
give birth to enduring love and tender compassion,
as they prepare for the lifelong bond of marriage.

May their families support them,
their friends encourage them,
and your holy people welcome them
as signs of your kindness and grace.

We ask this through Jesus Christ our Lord.

All: Amen.

For alternative prayers, see pages 14-16.

THE LORD'S PRAYER

The leader introduces the Lord's Prayer in these or similar words.

Leader: Now let us offer together the prayer
our Lord Jesus Christ taught us:

All: Our Father....

SIGN OF PEACE

The leader may invite all to exchange a sign of peace.

BLESSING OF FOOD AND DRINK (GRACE)

Since the meal takes place at the conclusion of this celebration, the following blessing may be used.

Leader: Blessed are you, Lord God of all creation,
who brings forth bread from the earth
and gives wine to gladden our hearts.
May the companionship we enjoy at this table
be the promise of a lifetime together.

We ask this through Christ our Lord.

All: Amen.

TOAST

During or at the end of the meal, one of those present may propose a toast to the couple.

PRAYERS BY THE ENGAGED COUPLE

Prayer of a Future Husband

Blessed are you, O God of our ancestors,
and blessed too is your name for ever.
Let the heavens bless you for evermore
and all the things you have made.

It was you who created Adam,
you who created Eve his wife
as a helper and support;
and from these two the human race was born.
It was you who said,
"It is not good that the man should be alone;
let us make him a helpmate like himself."

I take *N.*
in sincerity of heart.
Have mercy on her and on me
and bring us to old age together.

Have mercy on us, O Lord, have mercy on us:
and let us both grow old together in health.

cf. Adapted from *Tobit* 8.5-7.

Prayer of a Future Wife

Preserve me, God, I take refuge in you.
I say to the Lord:
"You are my God. My happiness lies in you alone."

You have put into my heart a marvellous love
for the faithful ones who dwell in your land.

O Lord, it is you who are my portion and cup;
it is you yourself who are my prize.
The lot marked out for me is my delight:
welcome indeed the heritage that falls to me!

I will bless the Lord who gives me counsel,
who even at night directs my heart.
I keep the Lord ever in my sight:
with God at my right hand, I shall stand firm.
And so my heart rejoices, my soul is glad;
even my body shall rest in safety.

You will show me the path of life,
the fullness of joy in your presence,
at your right hand happiness for ever.

cf. Adapted from *Psalm* 16.

Prayers for the Engaged Couple

Leader: Out of his infinite glory,
may God give you the power through his Spirit
for your hidden self to grow strong,
so that Christ may live in your hearts through faith,
and then, rooted and grounded in love,
you will with all the saints have strength
to grasp the breadth and the length,
the height and the depth;
until, knowing the love of Christ,
which is beyond all knowledge,
you are filled with the utter fullness of God.

Glory be to him whose power, working in us,
can do infinitely more than we can ask or imagine;
glory be to him from generation to generation
in the Church and in Christ Jesus
for ever and ever.

cf. Ephesians 3.16-21

All: Amen.

Or:

Leader: What we ask God
is that through perfect wisdom
and spiritual understanding
you should reach the fullest knowledge of his will.
So you will be able to lead the kind of life
which the Lord expects of you,
a life acceptable to him in all its aspects,
showing results in all the good actions you do
and increasing your knowledge of God.

You will have in you the strength,
based on his own glorious power,
never to give in, but to bear anything joyfully,
thanking the Father who has made it possible for you
to join the saints and with them to inherit the light.

Because that is what God has done:
he has taken us out of the power of darkness
and created a place for us
in the kingdom of the Son that he loves.

cf. *Colossians* 1.9-14

All: Amen.

Or:

Leader: May the Lord be generous in increasing your love
and make you love one another
and all humanity
as much as we love you.
May he so confirm your hearts in holiness
that you may be blameless
in the sight of our God and Father
when our Lord Jesus Christ comes with all his saints.

cf. *1 Thessalonians* 3.12-13

All: Amen.

Or:

Leader: I pray that the God of peace,
who brought our Lord Jesus back from the dead
to become the great Shepherd of the sheep
by the blood that sealed an eternal covenant,
may make you ready to do his will
in any kind of good action
and turn us all into whatever is acceptable to himself
through Jesus Christ,
to whom be glory for ever and ever.

cf. *Hebrews* 13.20-21

All: Amen.

Or:

Engagement   15

Leader: May almighty God bless you,
and unite your hearts in the enduring bond of pure love.
May you be blessed in your children,
and may the love that you lavish on them
be returned a hundredfold.

May the peace of Christ
dwell always in your hearts and in your home;
may you have true friends to stand by you,
both in joy and in sorrow.
May you be ready with help and consolation
for all those who come to you in need;
and may the blessings
promised to the compassionate
descend in abundance on your house.

May you be blessed in your work
and may it give you satisfaction.
May cares never cause you distress,
nor the desire for earthly possessions lead you astray;
but may your hearts' concern be always
for the treasures laid up for you in the life of heaven.

May the Lord grant you fullness of years,
so that you may reap the harvest of a good life,
and after you have served loyally
in his kingdom on earth
then may he take you up
into his eternal dominions in heaven.

And may the Lord be with you
now and always and for ever.

From an older ritual.

All: Amen.

AT MEAL BEFORE AND DURING WEDDING

AT A REHEARSAL SUPPER

Leader: God and Creator of us all,
we praise you and give you glory.
We thank you for the gifts you have given to us:
for the love you have shown *N.* and *N.*,
for the joy in their hearts today,
and for this supper we are about to share.

Bless us, O God, and the food we eat,
and make us truly grateful for all your gifts.

Give us grateful hearts to sing your praise,
now and for ever.

All: Amen.

AT A WEDDING BANQUET

Leader: God and Creator of us all,
you are the giver of all good gifts.

We praise and thank you today
for the love you have placed in the hearts of *N.* and *N.*,
and for allowing us to share in that love.
We thank you for the joy we feel
when we gather with friends.
We thank you for the food we are about to share.
Let this banquet be for us a sign of your constant care.

Bless us, and the food we eat.
Give us grateful hearts to sing your praise,
now and for ever.

All: Amen.

CELEBRATION OF A WEDDING ANNIVERSARY AT A FAMILY MEAL

Anniversaries are appropriately celebrated at a festive meal in the home. Before the meal begins, all gather in thanksgiving and prayer.

INVITATION TO PRAYER

When everyone is gathered at the table, the leader extends an invitation to spend a moment in quiet prayer.

Leader: Let us bless the Lord,
by whose goodness we live
and by whose grace we love one another.

Or:

Leader: We come together in joy this day
to celebrate the love of *N.* and *N.*.
Let us bless the Lord for their years together.

One of those present lights candles on the dining table.

Leader: May Christ dispel all darkness from our lives,
that together we may walk in light
and share the joy of life and love.
Blessed be God for ever.

All: Blessed be God for ever.

SCRIPTURE READING

One of those present reads a text from Scripture.
One of the following may be used.
The reading may begin in these or similar words.

Leader: Let us listen to these words from Scripture.

Reader: May the Lord make you increase
and abound in love for one another and for all,
just as we abound in love for you.
And may he so strengthen your hearts in holiness
that you may be blameless before our God and Father
at the coming of our Lord Jesus with all the saints.

1 Thessalonians 3.12-13

Or:

Reader: Love is patient; love is kind;
love is not envious or boastful or arrogant or rude.
It does not insist on its own way;
it is not irritable or resentful;
it does not rejoice in wrongdoing,
but rejoices in the truth.
It bears all things, believes all things,
hopes all things, endures all things.
Love never ends.

1 Corinthians 13.4-8a

Or:

Reader: Jesus said to his disciples,
"I give you a new commandment,
that you love one another.
Just as I have loved you,
you also should love one another.
By this everyone will know that you are my disciples,
if you have love for one another."

cf. *John* 13.34-35

Reflection

The leader or another person may offer a short reflection in which others, especially the couple (and their children), may also share.

Renewal of Commitment

The couple may wish to renew their commitment.
They join hands and say the following.
The couple speak in turn.

> *N.*, I renew the gift of myself to you;
> I renew the vow of my love.
> With all my heart I thank you;
> with all my love I embrace you.

Prayer for the Couple

The leader invites all to pray.
All may extend one or both hands over or toward the couple.

Leader: Blessed are you, Lord, loving God of all creation:
you have made us your beloved
and have showered gifts upon us.

We thank you for the life of *N.* and *N.*
and for their years together.
Continue to fill their hearts
with love for you and for each other.

Bless them (and their children)
and all their relatives and friends.
Lead us all through this life
to eternal happiness with you.

We ask this through Jesus Christ our Lord.

All: Amen.

The couple may kiss and share a sign of peace with those present.

BLESSING OF FOOD AND DRINK (GRACE)

The leader says one of the following prayers or another common or seasonal grace.

Leader: Generous God, giver of all good gifts,
we praise and thank you for *N.* and *N.*
and for allowing us to witness their love.
May the joy of this gathering and the food we share
be signs to us of your constant love.
Bless us and the food we eat
and give us grateful hearts to sing your praise
now and for ever.

All: Amen.

Or:

Leader: God of heaven and earth,
you give food and drink
to sustain our lives and gladden our hearts.
May we always be thankful for your providence
and mindful of the needs of others.
Give us grateful hearts to sing your praise
now and for ever.

All: Amen.

TOAST

During or at the end of the meal, one of those present may propose a toast to the couple.

Blessing God
in New Beginnings
and Birth / Initiation

HOME

A NEW HOME
(longer version)

When a family moves into a new home or apartment, they may invite the parish priest to join them and bless their new dwelling. If this is not possible or even before the formal blessing of their new residence, the family may gather in prayer to thank God for their new home and God's presence.

INTRODUCTION

Guests and friends may gather with the members of the family in a convenient location, such as a family or living room.

All make the sign of the cross as the leader begins:

Leader: In the name of the Father, and of the Son, ✠
and of the Holy Spirit.

All: Amen.

Leader: Peace be with this house and with all who live here.

All: May the peace of Christ dwell with us forever.

Or:

Leader: Peace to this house.

All: And to all who live here.

The leader may use these words to introduce the prayer service.

Leader: When Jesus took flesh through the Blessed Virgin Mary,
he made his home with us.
Now we pray that Christ will enter this (our) home
and bless it with his presence.
May he always be here among us
to nurture our love for each other,
to share in our joys and comfort us in our sorrows.
Inspired by his teachings and example,
let us seek to make this dwelling a place of love,
reflecting to all people the goodness of Christ.

SCRIPTURE READING

One or more of the following passages may be used.

Leader: Let us listen to these words from Scripture.

Reader: The mother of Jesus and his brothers came;
and standing outside,
they sent to him and called him.
A crowd was sitting around him;
and they said to him,
"Your mother and your brothers and sisters
are outside, asking for you."
And Jesus replied,
"Who are my mother and my brothers?"
And looking at those who sat around him, he said,
"Here are my mother and my brothers!
Whoever does the will of God
is my brother and sister and mother."

cf. *Mark* 3.31-35

Or:

Reader: For in him
all the fullness of God was pleased to dwell,
and through him
God was pleased to reconcile to himself
all things, whether on earth or in heaven,
by making peace through the blood of his cross.

And you who were once estranged
and hostile in mind, doing evil deeds,
he has now reconciled
in his fleshly body through death,
so as to present you holy and blameless
and irreproachable before him.

Colossians 1.19-22

Or:

Reader: This is his commandment, that we should believe
in the name of his Son Jesus Christ
and love one another, just as he has commanded us.

All who obey his commandments abide in him,
and he abides in them.
And by this we know that he abides in us,
by the Spirit that he has given us.

1 John 3.23-24

Or:

Other Passages:

Genesis	18.1-10 *the visit of God at the home of Abraham;*
Numbers	6.22-27 *the form of blessing;*
Matthew	5.1-12 *the Beatitudes* or 5.13-16 *salt of the earth and light of the world* or 10.11-15 *visiting a house or a town* or 12.18-21 *Jesus, the Lord's Servant, visiting the nations* or 18.1-5 *who is the greatest?* or 18.19-22 *prayer in common, forgiveness;*
Luke	10.5-9 *entering in a house* or 10.38-42 *Martha and Mary* or 19.1-9 *Zacchaeus;*
John	14.15-27 *to love Jesus and to receive his peace* or 15.1-17 *the true vine;*
Romans	12.1-8 *spiritual worship–humility and charity* or 12.9-16 *stick to what is good, keep praying* or 12.17-21 *charity to everyone, including enemies;*
1 Corinthians	12.4-12 *the variety and the unity of gifts* 12.31-13.7 *hymn to love;*
2 Corinthians	6.1-2 *now is the real time of favor;*

Galatians	1.3-5 *grace and peace from God to you;*
Ephesians	1.3-10 *God's plan of salvation* or 1.11-20 *the triumph and supremacy of Christ* or 3.14-21 *Paul's prayer* or 4.1-7 *a call to unity;*
Philippians	2.1-11 *preserve unity in humility* or 2.12-16 *work for salvation* or 4.4-9 *last advice;*
Colossians	1.9-14 *thanksgiving and prayer;*
1 John	4.4-12 *we are from God* or 4.13-21 *whoever remains in love remains in God* or 4.7-14 *the source of love.*

INTERCESSIONS OR LITANY

The leader introduces the intercessions, in these or similar words.

Leader: The Son of God, the Lord of heaven and earth,
made his home among us.
With praise and thanksgiving
let us call upon our God.

All: R. Lord, hear our prayer.

Another person announces the intentions.

Reader: That the home life of all Christians may be sanctified,
we pray. R.

That all believers may be holy temples of God's
presence, we pray. R.

That all people and nations may live in peaceful
co-existence, we pray. R.

That all men and women may serve with their whole
heart, we pray. R.

That we may comfort the sorrowing and welcome the
homeless, we pray. R.

That the sick may be cheered by our concern and our
visits, we pray. R.

That the departed may be welcomed into paradise,
we pray. R.

Or:

Reader: That the Lord will dwell in this home and enrich all who live here. R.

That the Church will be built up as the Body of Christ and dwelling place of the Spirit. R.

That all Christians will build their homes upon the solid rock of faith in Jesus. R.

That the world will be freed of discord, poverty and injustice. R.

That the homeless, the imprisoned and the exiled will know the warmth of God's presence. R.

That those who have died will come to the eternal banquet in God's kingdom. R.

Or:

All may pray the Litany of the Saints, see page 338-341.

PRAYER

The leader may conclude the intercessions with one of the following prayers.

Leader: Lord Jesus Christ,
be close to us, your servants,
as we move into this home (today)
and ask for your blessing.
Be our shelter when we are at home,
our companion when we are away,
and our welcome guest when we return.
Receive us at last
into the dwelling place you have prepared for us
in your Father's house,
where you live for ever and ever.

All: Amen.

Or:

Leader: Blessed are you, Lord God of all creation:
you have shared your life and grace with us.
In your mercy bless all who live here
(and our family and friends).
May this house be a place of prayer and peace.
May all who live here remain in your love,
and be generous in their love and service for others.
May the love of Jesus, Mary and Joseph,
and all your saints
inspire us to follow the example of your Son, Jesus,
who lives and reigns for ever and ever.

All: Amen.

PROCESSION THROUGH THE HOUSE
AND SPRINKLING OF BLESSED WATER

The leader may sprinkle those present and the new home with holy water.

Leader: Let this water call to mind our baptism into Christ,
who has redeemed us by his death and resurrection.

*All may go from room to room, offering prayers and sprinkling blessed water.
Some of the following prayers may be used, as seems appropriate.*

At the Entrance

Leader: Lord God, protect our going and coming;
let us share the hospitality of this home
with all who come to visit us.
Grant that all who enter here
may come to know your love and peace.

Grant this through Christ our Lord.

All: Amen.

In the Family or Living Room

Leader: O God,
as we gather in this room to share friendship,
be present to us
and bind us together in love and peace.

Grant this through Christ our Lord.

All: Amen.

In the Kitchen

Leader: O Lord, you fill the hungry with good things.
Send your blessing on us
as we work in this kitchen,
worrying about what we will eat and drink.
Teach us to share with others
what we receive from your Providence
in the spirit of thankfulness.

Grant this through Christ our Lord.

All: Amen.

See *Matthew* 6.25-33

In the Dining Room

Leader: Blessed are you, Lord God of heaven and earth,
for you give us food and drink to sustain our lives.
At this table, may we be grateful for all your gifts,
eat our food with glad and generous hearts
and be mindful of the needs of others.

Grant this through Christ our Lord.

All: Amen.

See *Acts* 2.46

In the Bedroom(s)

Leader: Protect us, Lord, as we stay awake;
watch over us as we sleep,
that awake, we may keep watch with Christ,
and asleep, we may rest in his peace.

Grant this through the same Christ our Lord.

All: Amen.

See antiphon to the Canticle of Simeon (page 90).

In the Bathroom

Leader: Blessed are you, Lord of heaven and earth
for you have formed us in your image
and renewed us in body and spirit through baptism.
Keep us in good health, as in this room
we will wash, like Jesus, feet, hands, and head
that we may be cleansed
to worthily serve you in each other.

Grant this through Christ our Lord.

All: Amen.

See *John* 13.9, 13-14

All return to the starting place where a cross or icon may be placed in a permanent place of honor (see next page).

PLACING OF A CROSS OR ICON

If desired, a cross or icon may be placed in a permanent place of honor at this time or at a later date. A candle may be lighted before it. Each person may hold the cross or icon, bless themselves with it, or venerate it in some way.

For a Cross

Leader: Almighty God,
you sent your Son to us because you love all people,
and want them to be saved.
By the power of his Cross,
free us from sin and let us live each day for you.
We bless and praise you for this sign of glory.
Let this cross remind us
that Jesus died and rose for all.
Help us to carry our cross with him every day,
that we may follow him in serving others
and living the new life he won for all.

We ask this through Jesus Christ our Lord.

All: Amen.

For an Icon or Image of Christ

Leader: Holy God,
you love us and call us to be your holy people.
We praise and bless you for this image of your Son;
grant us your strength and protection
that we may imitate his love for you
and his service of others.
Bring us to share in the joy of your Spirit.

We ask this through Jesus Christ our Lord.

All: Amen.

For an Icon or Image of Mary

Leader: All praise and glory are yours, Lord,
you have given us your Son to save us from sin.
We praise you for choosing Mary to be his mother,
for teaching her to believe your message,
for helping her to accept your holy will.
May this image of Mary our mother
help us to draw inspiration from her
in loving and serving you.

We ask this through Jesus Christ our Lord.

All: Amen.

For an Icon or Image of a Saint

Leader: Lord our God,
you have called us to be your holy people.
Through the prayers and example of Saint N.,
help us to love you more fully
and serve you more faithfully.
We praise and bless you for the life of Saint N.;
let this image remind us of the love
he/she and all your saints had for you.

We ask this through Jesus Christ our Lord.

All: Amen.

Or:

Leader: Blessed are you, Lord God of all creation.
You are the source of all life and every blessing.
Be with us now and grant that
whenever we look upon this symbol of our faith
we may be transformed into the image of your Son,
who died to save us from our sins,
and rose to bring us new life,
and who lives and reigns with you
in the unity of the Holy Spirit,
God, for ever and ever.

All: Amen.

Concluding Rite

The leader introduces the Lord's Prayer in these or similar words.

Leader: Now let us offer together the prayer
our Lord Jesus Christ taught us:

All: Our Father....

The leader concludes.

Leader: May the peace of Christ rule in our hearts,
and may the word of Christ in all its richness
dwell in us,
so that whatever we do in word and work,
we will do in the name of the Lord.

All: Amen.

All may exchange the sign of peace.
If appropriate, all may share a meal together.

A HOME
(simpler version)

The leader may be a priest or other pastoral minister, a parent or friend.

GREETING

The couple and their guests gather in a suitable place. All make the sign of the cross as the leader says:

Leader: Peace be to this house and all who will live here.
Blessed be God for ever.

All: Blessed be God for ever.

INTRODUCTION

The leader may introduce the celebration, using these or similar words.

Leader: My dear friends,
let us now pray that the Lord will enter this home
and bless it with his presence.
May the Lord always be here among you,
deepen your love for each other,
share in your joys,
and comfort you in your sorrows.
May your (new) home be a place of love,
filled with the goodness of the Lord.

Scripture Reading

One of the following passages of Scripture is read.

Leader: Let us listen to these words from Scripture.

Reader: As Jesus and his disciples went on their way,
he entered a certain village,
where a woman named Martha
welcomed him into her home.
She had a sister named Mary,
who sat at the Lord's feet
and listened to what he was saying.
But Martha was distracted by her many tasks;
so she came to him and asked,
"Lord, do you not care
that my sister has left me to do all the work by myself?
Tell her then to help me."
But the Lord answered her,
"Martha, Martha,
you are worried and distracted by many things;
there is need of only one thing.
Mary has chosen the better part,
which will not be taken away from her."

Luke 10.38-42

Or:

Reader: Jesus entered Jericho and was passing through it.
A man was there named Zacchaeus;
he was a chief tax collector and was rich.
He was trying to see who Jesus was,
but on account of the crowd he could not,
because he was short in stature.
So he ran ahead
and climbed a sycamore tree to see him,
because he was going to pass that way.
When Jesus came to the place,
he looked up and said to him,
"Zacchaeus, hurry and come down;
for I must stay at your house today."

So he hurried down and was happy to welcome him.
All who saw it began to grumble and said,
"He has gone to be the guest of one who is a sinner."
Zacchaeus stood there and said to the Lord,
"Look, half of my possessions, Lord,
I will give to the poor;
and if I have defrauded anyone of anything,
I will pay back four times as much."
Then Jesus said to him,
"Today salvation has come to this house,
because he too is a son of Abraham."

Luke 19.1-9

Or:

Reader: John [the Baptist]
was standing with two of his disciples,
and as he watched Jesus walk by, he exclaimed,
"Look, here is the Lamb of God!"
The two disciples heard him say this,
and they followed Jesus.
When Jesus turned and saw them following,
he said to them,
"What are you looking for?"
They said to him, "Rabbi"
(which translated means Teacher),
"where are you staying?"
He said to them, "Come and see."
They came and saw where he was staying,
and they remained with him that day.

John 1.35-39

REFLECTION

The leader may offer a few words of reflection on the reading and its
relationship to the life of the couple. The couple and others present may add
further reflections.

PRAYER OF BLESSING

The leader says one of the following prayers.

Leader: Blessed are you, Lord God,
you have shared your life and grace with this family.
In your mercy
bless them and bless their home.
May they be people of prayer,
and their home a place of prayer and peace.
Let them live in your love,
and be generous in their love and service for others.
May the faith of Mary and Joseph and all your saints
inspire them to follow the example of your Son, Jesus,
who is our Lord and Saviour for ever and ever.

All: Amen.

Or:

Leader: O God,
you have created us in love and saved us in mercy.
Through the bond of marriage
you have established the family
and willed that it should become a sign
of Christ's love for his Church.
Shower your blessings on this family
gathered here in your name.
Enable those who are joined by one love
to support one another
by their fervor of spirit and devotion to prayer.
Make them responsive to the needs of others
and witnesses to the faith in all they say and do.

We ask this through Christ our Lord.

All: Amen.

Or:

Leader: Lord, Jesus Christ,
bless your servants *N.* and *N.*
as they begin their life together in this home.
Be their shelter when they are here,
their companion when they are away,
and their welcome guest when they return.
At the last receive them
into the dwelling place you have prepared for them
in your Father's house
where you live for ever and ever.

All: Amen.

When a priest or deacon is the leader, he may bless water using the following
words:

Bless ✠ this water, Lord,
and let it remind us of our baptism.
Help us to live as people of light
and to be blameless and worthy in your sight.

The leader may sprinkle the house and those present with holy water.

THE LORD'S PRAYER

The leader introduces the Lord's Prayer in these or similar words.

Leader: Now let us offer together the prayer
our Lord Jesus Christ taught us:

All: Our Father....

Concluding Rite

The leader concludes by saying one of the following.

Leader: May the peace of Christ rule in our hearts,
and may the word of Christ in all its richness
dwell in us,
so that whatever we do in word and in work
we will do in the name of the Lord.

All: Amen.

Or:

Leader: May the Lord bless us,
as he once blessed our ancestors in faith.
May God's hand be over us,
and may he send his holy angel
to protect us all the days of our life.

All: Amen.

The leader may invite all to exchange a sign of peace.

WELCOMING LIFE

PREGNANCY

These prayers may be used at home throughout the time of pregnancy. They may be added to the Meal Prayers or Daily Praise from time to time.

INTRODUCTION

If there are children present, one of the parents may explain the significance of the occasion and the joy they feel; how the family blesses and praises God for this good news and asks for God's protection, especially for the mother and child.

> The leader then invites all to pray.
> All make the sign of the cross as the leader begins:

Leader: In the name of the Father, and of the Son, ✠
and of the Holy Spirit.

All: Amen.

Leader: Today we praise God
for the new gift of life he has given us (this family).

We join in prayer for *N.* and her child,
and ask God to protect them.

Scripture Reading

One of the following passages is read.

Leader: Let us listen to these words from Scripture.

Reader: People were bringing the little children to Jesus
in order that he might touch them;
and the disciples spoke sternly to them.
But when Jesus saw this,
he was indignant and said to them,
"Let the little children come to me;
do not stop them;
for it is to such as these
that the kingdom of God belongs.
Truly I tell you,
whoever does not receive the kingdom of God
as a little child will never enter it."

And he took them up in his arms,
and laid his hands on them, and blessed them.

Mark 10.13-16

Or:

Reader: Everyone who believes
that Jesus is the Christ has been born of God,
and everyone who loves the parent loves the child.
By this we know that we love the children of God,
when we love God and obey his commandments.

For the love of God is this,
that we obey his commandments.
And his commandments are not burdensome,
for whatever is born of God conquers the world.
And this is the victory that conquers the world,
our faith.

Who is it that conquers the world
but the one who believes
that Jesus is the Son of God?

1 John 5.1-5

Or:

Other Passages:

Mark	9.33-37 *who is the greatest?*
Luke	1.39-45 *the visitation* or 1.46-56 *my soul proclaims the greatness of the Lord;* or 2.1-7 *the birth of Jesus* or 2.8-21 *the visit of the shepherds at the birth of Jesus;*
Ephesians	3.14-21 *Paul's prayer;*
Colossians	1.9-14 *lead a life worthy of the Lord;* or 3.12-17 *bear with one another;*
1 John	4.7-21 *the source of love.*

INTERCESSIONS

The leader introduces the intercessions.

Leader: Bless us as we gather here, Lord,
to celebrate your gift of life.

All: R. Lord, hear our prayer.

Another person announces the intentions.

Reader: Look with love upon N. and N.
and their unborn child. R.

Grant that this child may come to a safe birth. R.

May this child be strong and healthy. R.

Bring this child to new life in baptism. R.

(May their children embrace this new sibling
with love and joy. R.)

Guide this family
as they raise their child (children) in your love. R.

Bless all the families in our community. R.

Or:

Parent: Bless us as we gather here, Lord,
to celebrate your gift of life.

All: R. Lord, hear our prayer.

Parent: Look with love upon N. (my wife/this mother)
and our child. R.

Grant that our child may come to a safe birth. R.

May our child be strong and healthy. R.

Bring our child to new life in baptism. R.

(May our children embrace this new child
with love and joy. R.)

Guide our family as we raise our child (children) in
your love. R.

Bless all the families in our community. R.

PRAYER

One of the following prayers concludes the intercessions.

For the Mother

Leader: Loving God,
we rejoice in the gift of life that you have given to N..
Look with love upon her and her child:
pour out your blessing upon her
and guide her throughout life.

Grant that her child will grow in wisdom, age,
and grace in your presence and before all your people.

We praise you, God of all life, and ask this grace
through Jesus Christ our Lord.

All: Amen.

For the Mother and Father

Leader: Lord God, creator of all life,
we praise you that you have given life to this child,
and we rejoice with these parents
as they prepare for the birth of their child.

Protect *N.* as she carries her child in her womb,
and bring her to a safe delivery.
May their child be baptized into the life of Jesus,
and live always in a way pleasing to you.

We ask this through Jesus Christ our Lord.

All: Amen.

By the Father

Father: Heavenly Father, creator of all life,
we praise you that you have given life to our child,
and we rejoice with our family and friends
as we prepare for its birth.

Protect (my wife,) *N.*,
as she carries our child in her womb,
and bring her to a safe delivery.

May our child be baptized into the life of Jesus,
and live in the community of your people,
and proclaim your praise and glory.

We ask this through Jesus Christ our Lord.

All: Amen.

Or:

Father: Loving Father,
we rejoice in the gift of life
that you have given to me and my wife.
We ask you to look with love upon us and our child:
pour out your blessing upon us
and guide us all the days of our lives.

Grant that this child will grow
in wisdom, age, and grace
in your presence and before all your people.

We praise you, God of all life,
and ask this grace through Jesus Christ our Lord.

All: Amen.

Or:

Father: May God bless and protect us,
and bring our child to a safe birth.

All: Amen.

Prayer by the Parents

Parents: Lord God, giver of all good gifts,
we thank you that you have called husband and wife
to be one in mind and heart and love
and to be a sign of Christ's love for the Church.

We thank you for the fruit of our love
and pray for ourselves and for all husbands and wives
who are called to be parents.
We praise you for this blessing
and ask you to be with us
in this moment of joy and awe,
as we face the challenges of parenthood.

Fill us with your unconditional love
and sustain us always with your mercy,
that our lives may reflect Christ's love for us
and lead our family to proclaim your greatness
in the midst of your Church.

Glory and honor and praise be yours, Lord God,
through Jesus Christ our Lord,
in the power of the Holy Spirit,
now and always and for ever.

All: Amen.

Prayer with Children

This prayer may also be said by older children.

Leader: All praise and glory is yours, almighty God,
for you have given our family
the joy of another member.

Open our arms and hearts
to embrace this new child.
Let the life in mom's (my) womb
bring us to experience the mystery of your life
and know the joy of your presence among us.

Bless our (us) children;
help them (us) to be brothers and sisters to this new child
as your Son Jesus was a brother to us
and loved all children.

All glory and praise are yours, Lord,
for ever and ever.

All: Amen.

Or:

Leader: All praise to you, Lord Jesus,
lover of children.
Bless our children,
and help us to lead them to you.

All glory and praise are yours, Lord,
for ever and ever.

All: Amen.

Conclusion

As a reminder of baptism, the leader may sprinkle all with blessed water, or they may take it and make the sign of the cross.

Leader: Let us use this blessed water
as a reminder of our baptism,
and with the prayer that our (this) child
will share with us
in the wonderful blessings of Christian life.

The leader invites all to say the Lord's Prayer.

Leader: Let us pray together the prayer that Jesus taught us:

All: Our Father....

Leader: May almighty God order our days and our deeds
in his peace.

All: Amen.

All may exchange a sign of peace.

Birth or Adoption of a Child

After a baby has been born, or the parents have received an adopted child, all may thank God for a safe arrival.

This prayer may be said by the family at the hospital in the prayer or quiet room, when the family gathers with the mother, or when the new child is brought home for the first time.

Introduction

Guests and friends gather with the members of the family.
All make the sign of the cross as the leader begins:

Leader: In the name of the Father, and of the Son, ✠ and of the Holy Spirit.

All: Amen.

Scripture Reading

All listen as a gospel passage is read.

Leader: Let us listen to these words from Scripture.

Reader: The disciples came to Jesus and asked, "Who is the greatest in the kingdom of heaven?"

He called a child, whom he put among them, and said, "Truly I tell you,
unless you change and become like children,
you will never enter the kingdom of heaven.
Whoever becomes humble like this child
is the greatest in the kingdom of heaven.
Whoever welcomes one such child in my name
welcomes me."

Matthew 18.1-4

Or:

Reader: People were bringing the little children to Jesus
in order that he might touch them;
and the disciples spoke sternly to them.

But when Jesus saw this,
he was indignant and said to them,
"Let the little children come to me;
do not stop them;
for it is to such as these
that the kingdom of God belongs.
Truly I tell you,
whoever does not receive the kingdom of God
as a little child will never enter it."

And he took them up in his arms,
laid his hands on them, and blessed them.

Mark 10.13-16

Or:

Reader: An argument arose among the disciples
as to which one was the greatest.

But Jesus, aware of their inner thoughts,
took a little child and put it by his side,
and said to them,
"Whoever welcomes this child in my name
welcomes me,
and whoever welcomes me
welcomes the one who sent me;
for the least among all of you is the greatest."

Luke 9.46-48

Or:

Other Passages:

Matthew	19.13-15 *Jesus and the children;*
Mark	9.33-37 *who is the greatest;* or 10.13-16 *Jesus and the children;*
Luke	18.15-17 *Jesus and the children.*

Intercession – Litany

The baptismal litany (pages 63-64), the litany of the saints (pages 338-341), or the following short litany may be said.

Leader: Lord, have mercy.

All: Lord, have mercy.

Leader: Christ, have mercy.

All: Christ, have mercy.

Leader: Lord, have mercy.

All: Lord, have mercy.

Leader: Holy Mary, Mother of God,

All: pray for us.

Leader: Saint Joseph,

All: pray for us.

Leader: Saint John the Baptist,

All: pray for us.

Leader: Saint Peter and Saint Paul,

All: pray for us.

The names of other saints may be included here.

Leader: All holy men and women,

All: pray for us.

Or:

Leader: Lord God, bless *N.* in your love.

All: *R.* Lord, hear our prayer.

Leader: Bless *N.* and *N.* as they accept their new child. *R.*

Show him/her your goodness through the love
of his/her parents. *R.*

Bless their home, and make their family happy
in your service. *R.*

Other petitions may be added by those who have gathered for the celebration.

Or:

Leader: Lord God, bless us, and our families and friends.

All: *R.* Lord, hear our prayer.

Leader: Look upon us in your love. *R.*

Show us your mercy and love. *R.*

Support us through the love of our families
and friends. *R.*

Protect us from sin and harm. *R.*

Guide us with your light. *R.*

Lead us to your kingdom. *R.*

Other petitions may be added by those who have gathered for the celebration.

PRAYER OF PRAISE

One of the following prayers may conclude the intercessions or litany.

Leader: Blessed are you, Lord God of all creation:
you have given us joy in the birth (arrival)
of this (our) child.
We rejoice (with our family and friends,)
and proclaim the greatness of your name.

Grant that *N.* will be strong and healthy.
Bring him/her to the grace of baptism,
so that he/she may grow to full maturity in Christ,
be a member of your holy people,
and a source of strength and encouragement for all.

Lord God,
we bless and praise you for this happy day;
we glorify you for the wisdom of your Son
and the grace of your Holy Spirit;
we rejoice with all the Church and all your people
and offer you praise through Jesus Christ our Lord.

All: Amen.

For a Baptized Child

Leader: Blessed are you, Lord God,
maker of the universe and Father of all:
you have made us your children,
brothers and sisters of Jesus,
and temples of your Holy Spirit.
You invite us to call you Father
in the community of your holy people.
Hear the prayers we make this day
as we rejoice in your love
and welcome *N.* into our family.

Fill our home with your peace
and lead us always in your love.
Blessed are you, Lord our God, for ever and ever.

All: Amen.

Or:

Leader: Loving God,
you have chosen each one of us
and called us by name
to be your son(s) and/or daughter(s)
and to live in your kingdom.

By the power of the Holy Spirit,
move us to use our gifts
for the building up your Church.

Inspire each of us to thank you every day
for the gift of life you share with us.
Teach us to accept our own limitations,
and to develop all the abilities we have.
Help us to be patient with ourselves and others,
and to work together to make this
a better world for all people.

Give your special blessing to *N.*,
our son/daughter,
and help him/her to grow in your love
and to serve you each day.

We make our prayer through our Lord Jesus Christ,
in the love of the Holy Spirit,
one God, for ever and ever.

All: Amen.

For an Older Child

Leader: Heavenly Father, lover of all,
we praise you for giving us Jesus as our Savior:
he blessed the children who came to him,
and welcomes those who come to him now.

Look with favor upon *N.*, our son/daughter,
and embrace him/her with your love.
May he/she grow in assurance of our love,
in the wisdom and knowledge of your Son, Jesus,
and in the strength of the Holy Spirit.
May he/she be one with us
as we praise you for your presence.

We ask this through your beloved Son,
Jesus Christ our Lord.

All: Amen.

Or:

Leader: Praise to you, Lord Jesus,
lover of children.
Bless the little ones in our family,
and help us to lead them to you.

All glory and praise are yours for ever and ever.

All: Amen.

CONCLUSION

The leader invites all to say the Lord's Prayer.

Leader: Disciples of Christ,
we also are members of a larger family, the Church.
Let us (join our hands and) pray together
with the words our Savior taught us:

All: Our Father....

Then all may exchange a sign of peace.

Birthday
and / or
Name Day

A member of the family may lead this prayer service at the party or gathering with friends and family or at another time.

Introduction

Guests and friends gather with the members of the family.
All make the sign of the cross as the leader begins:

Leader: In the name of the Father, and of the Son, ✠ and of the Holy Spirit.

All: Amen.

Scripture Reading

All listen as a Scripture passage is read.

Leader: Let us listen to these words from Scripture.

Reader: Now the word of the Lord came to me saying,
          "Before I formed you in the womb I knew you,
          and before you were born I consecrated you."

Jeremiah 1.4-5a

Or:

Reader: The one who enters by the gate
          is the shepherd of the sheep.
          The gatekeeper opens the gate for him,
          and the sheep hear his voice.
          He calls his own sheep by name and leads them out.
          When he has brought out all his own,
          he goes ahead of them,
          and the sheep follow him because they know his voice.

John 10.2-4

LITANY

The leader invites all to pray together.

Leader: God of love, we thank you for the life of *N.*.

All: *R.* Glory and praise forever.

We thank you for all his/her family and friends
gathered here. *R.*

We thank you for keeping us safe in your love. *R.*

We thank you for the years
you have given him/her. *R.*

We thank you for keeping him/her in your sight. *R.*

We thank you for the intercession
of Saint *N.* (patron saint),
guiding this child in your way. *R.*

PRAYER

The leader concludes the litany with one of the following prayers.
A specific prayer to the Patron Saint of the one who is surrounded by those
gathered in this moment of prayer, if available, may also be used.

Leader: May God bless you with every good gift
and surround you with love and happiness this day.
May Jesus Christ, the only Son of God,
be your friend and guide all the days of your life.
May the Spirit of God lead you,
and guide your footsteps in the path of Jesus,
who loved us and died for our sins.

All: Amen.

Or:

For a Child at a Birthday Party

Leader: Lord Jesus, our brother,
you love us all,
and have a special love for the young.
Bless N. on his/her birthday,
and help him/her to be happy
and always pleasing to you.
Bless all of us, Lord Jesus,
as we celebrate this happy occasion.
You are Lord for ever and ever.

All: Amen.

Leader: Saint N. (patron saint),

All: Pray for us.

Or:

For an Adult

Leader: Heavenly Father,
we praise you for all your gifts to us.
In a special way, we thank you for N..
Bless him/her on this birthday,
and keep him/her always in your love.
Bless us too, holy God,
(and this food with which we celebrate).

May we praise you and give you glory
through Jesus Christ our Lord.

All: Amen.

Leader: Saint N. (patron saint),

All: Pray for us.

Or:

For an Elderly Person

Leader: Heavenly Father,
remember *N.* who loves you
and who has grown old in your service.
Bless him/her on this birthday,
and give him/her strength and courage
to follow you.
Keep *N.* in your love.
Give him/her joy and peace each day.

May we praise you and give you glory
through Jesus Christ our Lord.

All: Amen.

Leader: Saint *N.* (patron saint),

All: Pray for us.

CONCLUSION

All may exchange a sign of peace.

WELCOMING CHRISTIAN LIFE

BAPTISM

In the period between the birth of a child and the celebration of baptism, parents (and godparents) are invited to celebrate the new life in Christ for their child that they will eventually celebrate sacramentally in baptism.

INTRODUCTION

At the beginning of the celebration, the parents are asked to state their own commitment in the days before the baptism.

Leader: You have asked to have your children baptized.
In doing so you are accepting the responsibility
of training them in the practice of the faith.
It will be your duty to bring them up
to keep God's commandments as Christ taught us,
by loving God and our neighbor.

SCRIPTURE READING

Passages from the liturgy of baptism may be used for refection and prayer.

Leader: In Christ Jesus
you are all children of God through faith.
As many of you as were baptized into Christ
have clothed yourselves with Christ.
There is no longer Jew or Greek,
there is no longer slave or free,
there is no longer male and female;
for all of you are one in Christ Jesus.

Galatians 3.26-28

Or:

Other Passages:

Ezekiel   36.24-28 *I shall pour clean water over you. I shall put my spirit in you;* or
               47.1-9, 12 *the spring in the Temple;*

Romans   6.3-5 *our baptism;* or 8.28-32 *God has called us to share his glory;*

1 Corinthians 12.12-13 *we were baptized into one body in a single Spirit;*

Colossians   3.12-17 *you are the chosen of God;*

Ephesians   4.1-6 *a call to unity;*

1 Peter   2.4-5, 9-10 *the new priesthood;*

Matthew   22.35-40 *the greatest commandment of all;* or 28.18-20 *baptize all nations;*

Mark   1.9-11 *Jesus is baptized;* or 10.13-16 *Jesus and the children;* or 12.28b-34
               the greatest commandment of all;

John   3.1-6 *being born through water and the Spirit;* or 4.5-14 *the Samaritan
               woman and the living water;* or 6.44-47 *everyone who believes has eternal
               life;* or 7.37b-39a *the promise of living water;* or 9.1-7 the cure of the man
               born blind;* or 15.1-11 *the true vine;* or 19.31-35 *the pierced Christ.*

PROFESSION OF FAITH

Parents and godparents may also reflect upon the profession of faith made at their own baptism that they will renew at the baptism of their child. The leader may first explain some of the main statements of our profession of faith (reject evil, choose good; faith in the Trinity).

The leader may then ask:

Leader: Do you reject sin,
         so as to live in the freedom of God's children?

All: I do.

Leader: Do you reject the glamour of evil,
         and refuse to be mastered by sin?

All: I do.

Leader: Do you reject Satan,
         father of sin and prince of darkness?

All: I do.

Leader: Do you believe in God, the Father almighty,
creator of heaven and earth?

All: I do.

Leader: Do you believe in Jesus Christ, his only Son, our Lord,
who was born of the Virgin Mary,
was crucified, died and was buried,
rose from the dead,
and is now seated at the right hand of the Father?

All: I do.

Leader: Do you believe in the Holy Spirit,
the holy catholic Church, the communion of saints,
the forgiveness of sins, the resurrection of the body,
and the life everlasting?

All: I do.

LITANY IN PREPARATION FOR BAPTISM

Leader: Lord, have mercy.

All: Lord, have mercy.

Leader: Christ, have mercy.

All: Christ, have mercy.

Leader: Lord, have mercy.

All: Lord, have mercy.

Leader: Holy Mary, Mother of God,

All: pray for us.

Leader: St. Joseph,

All: pray for us.

Leader: St. John the Baptist,

All: pray for us.

Leader: St. Peter and St. Paul,

All: pray for us.

Leader: St. Joachim and St. Anne,

All: pray for us.

In the United States:

Leader: Isaac Jogues and St. René Goupil

All: pray for us.

Leader: St. John Neumann

All: pray for us.

Leader: St. Elizabeth Ann Seton, St. Rose Philippine Duchesne,
St. Mother Théodore Guérin,
St. Frances Xavier Cabrini, St. Katharine Drexel

All: pray for us.

The names of other saints may be added, especially the patron of the church, of the child to be baptized, and his/her parents.

The litany concludes:

Leader: All holy men and women,

All: pray for us.

Leader: God of new beginnings,
          Creator of heaven and earth,
          you made us in your image and likeness,
          and blessed us
          so that we may become stewards of your creation.
          Through the intercession
          of holy men and women of all times,
          bless this child created according to your likeness
          and about to begin his/her Christian journey.
          May he/she walk faithfully
          in the path of your Son,
          witness the Gospel of love and mercy,
          and contribute with the work of his/her hands
          to make visible your Kingdom on earth.

          We ask this through the same Christ our Lord.

All: Amen.

Other prayers, from the Anniversary of Baptism, may also be used. See pages 70-72.

CONCLUSION

All may exchange a sign of peace.

Anniversary of Baptism

This prayer service may be used to express our personal and community thanks to God for having led us to him through Christian Initiation. It may be prayed at any time during the year, but is particularly suitable on Easter Sunday, during the Easter season, or on the exact date of baptism or initiation.

Introduction

Guests and friends may gather with the members of the family in a convenient location, such as a family or living room.

All make the sign of the cross as the leader begins:

Leader: In the name of the Father, and of the Son, ✠ and of the Holy Spirit.

All: Amen.

Scripture Reading

One of the readings from the baptismal liturgy may be proclaimed.

Leader: Let us listen to these words of Scripture.

Reader: Do you not know that all of us
who have been baptized into Christ Jesus
were baptized into his death?
Therefore we have been buried with him
by baptism into death,
so that, just as Christ was raised from the dead
by the glory of the Father,
so we too might walk in newness of life.

For if we have been united with him
in a death like his,
we will certainly be united with him
in a resurrection like his.

Romans 6.3-5

Or:

Reader: I therefore, the prisoner in the Lord,
          beg you to lead a life worthy of the calling
          to which you have been called,
          with all humility and gentleness,
          with patience, bearing with one another in love,
          making every effort
          to maintain the unity of the Spirit
          in the bond of peace.
          There is one body and one Spirit,
          just as you were called
          into the one hope of your calling,
          one Lord, one faith, one baptism,
          one God and Father of all,
          who is above all and through all and in all.

Ephesians 4.1-6

Or:

Reader: In those days Jesus came from Nazareth of Galilee
          and was baptized by John in the Jordan.
          And just as he was coming up out of the water,
          he saw the heavens torn apart
          and the Spirit descending like a dove on him.
          And a voice came from heaven,
          "You are my Son, the Beloved;
          with you I am well pleased."

Mark 1.9-11

Or:

Other Passages:

Ezekiel	36.24-28 *I shall pour clean water over you. I shall put my spirit in you;*
Romans	8.28-32 *God has called us to share his glory;*
1 Corinthians	12.12-13 *we were baptized into one body in a single Spirit;*
Colossians	3.12-17 *you are the chosen of God;*
1 Peter	2.4-5, 9-10 *the new priesthood;*
Matthew	28.18-20 *baptize all nations;*
John	3.1-6 *being born through water and the Spirit.*

INTERCESSIONS

The leader invites all to join in the intercessions.
Some of the following invocations may be used.
Other gifts may be mentioned in this litany of thanksgiving.

Leader: Lord God, you bless us with the gift of life.

All: R. We give you thanks and praise.

Another person may read the invocations.

Reader: You give us your Son as our Savior. R.

You teach us his words of life. R.

You make us your holy people. R.

You cleanse us from our sins. R.

You invite us to love you by loving others. R.

You give us talents to use for your glory. R.

You call us to do good works
in response to your gifts. R.

You nourish us with the bread of life. R.

You give us the cup of salvation. R.

You send us your Holy Spirit. R.

You promise us the joys of heaven. R.

You call us to sing your praises for ever. R.

Or:

The following may be used as a litany or prayer.

Leader: Lord Jesus Christ, we praise you:
for calling us to follow you,
for being our Lord and brother,
and for letting us share your cross.
(For all these gifts we say:

All: We give you thanks, O Lord.)

Leader: Lord our Savior, we thank you:
for sharing your life with us,
for leading us in your light,
and for sending your Spirit to live in us.
(For all these gifts we say:

All: We give you thanks, O Lord.)

Leader: Jesus our resurrection and life, we give you glory:
for baptizing us into your death,
for raising us to new life with you,
for calling us to be members of your kingdom.
(For all these gifts we say:

All: We give you thanks, O Lord.)

Leader: Jesus our Redeemer, we worship you:
for calling us to give you praise,
for sanctifying us as your holy people,
and for bringing us to eternal life with all the saints.
(For all these gifts we say:

All: We give you thanks, O Lord.)

Leader: Giver of the Spirit, we praise you:
for marking us with your seal of life,
for giving us faith and hope,
and for filling us with your love.
(For all these gifts we say:

All: We give you thanks, O Lord.)

Prayer of Praise

All may lay their hands in silent prayer on the head or shoulder of the one who is celebrating the anniversary.

The leader may conclude with one of the following prayers.

Leader: Blessed are you, Lord,
creator of the universe and God of covenant:
of old you chose Abraham and Sarah
to be our ancestors in faith.
You made a covenant with your beloved people Israel
and led them through the waters
to your promised land.

We praise you,
Lord of history, Father of our Lord Jesus Christ:
now you have made a new covenant with us
in Jesus your Son.
You seal your love in the gift of the Holy Spirit
and give us the pledge of eternal life.

Keep us firm in your love and faithful in your service.
Renew the wonders of your covenant
in the lives of all people
and lead us to the glory of your kingdom.

All glory and praise are yours,
all powerful and loving God,
through Jesus Christ our Lord,
in the love of your Holy Spirit,
now and always and for ever.

All: Amen.

Or:

Leader: Blessed are you, Lord God, ruler of all creation:
you have made us your beloved children,
brothers and sisters of Jesus our Savior
and temples of your Spirit.

We thank you for making us Christians:
for the grace that helps us die to sin
and live for your glory with Christ
in the strength of the Holy Spirit.

Lead all people into your kingdom of light
and give them a place at the banquet of eternal life
with all the saints in glory.

All praise and glory be to you,
holy Father, almighty and eternal God,
through your Son, Jesus Christ,
in the unity of your Holy Spirit,
now and always and for ever.

All: Amen.

Or:

Leader: All praise and glory are yours, Lord our God,
creator of the universe and Father of all:
we thank you for choosing us to be your people,
for adopting us as your children in Christ,
and for sending us your Spirit to lead us to you.

Lord God, we bless you and give you glory,
through Christ our Lord and our brother,
in the love of your Holy Spirit,
now and always and for ever.

All: Amen.

Or:

Leader: Blessed are you, Lord God of all creation:
we praise you for the love and mercy
which you have shown to all your people.

Today we give you thanks and glory
as we celebrate the anniversary of the day
when you made *N.* your son/daughter in baptism.

Give him/her the grace to live in your love,
and help this family to draw closer to you
by faith, prayer, and example.

All glory is yours, kind and merciful God,
through Jesus your Son,
in the communion of the Holy Spirit,
now and always and for ever.

All: Amen.

CONCLUSION

All may recite the Lord's Prayer and exchange a sign of peace.

Confirmation

In the days before the celebration of confirmation, candidates, their sponsors, and families are invited to celebrate the gift of the Spirit that they will receive in fullness in the sacrament.

The baptismal profession of faith (see Baptism, pages 62-63 and the Apostles' Creed, page 282) is expanded to reflect further on the Spirit.

> Do you believe in the Holy Spirit,
> the Lord, the giver of life,
> who came upon the apostles at Pentecost
> and who allows you to give witness to Christ?

Prayers from the Anniversary of Baptism may be used. See pages 70-72.

The following may be used for personal prayer or at a session in preparation for the sacrament.

Introduction

All gather in a convenient place, a family or living room.
All make the sign of the cross as the leader begins:

Leader: In the name of the Father, and of the Son, ✠
and of the Holy Spirit.

All: Amen.

Leader: Come, Holy Spirit, fill the hearts of your faithful.

All: Kindle in them the fire of your love.

Scripture Reading

One of the following readings may be proclaimed.

Leader: Let us listen to these words from Scripture.

Reader: Do you not know that all of us
who have been baptized into Christ Jesus
were baptized into his death?
Therefore, we have been buried with him
by baptism into death, so that,
just as Christ was raised from the dead
by the glory of the Father,
so too we might walk in newness of life.
For as we have been united with him
in a death like his,
we will certainly be united with him
in a resurrection like his.

Romans 6.3-5

Or:

Leader: For all who are led by the Spirit of God
are children of God.
For you did not receive a spirit of slavery
to fall back into fear,
but you have received a spirit of adoption.
When we cry "Abba! Father!"
it is that very Spirit bearing witness with our spirit
that we are children of God,
and if children, then heirs,
heirs of God and joint heirs with Christ –
if, in fact, we suffer with him
so that we may also be glorified with him.

Romans 8.14-17

Or:

Leader: In those days Jesus came from Nazareth of Galilee
and was baptized by John in the Jordan.
And just as he was coming up out of the water,
he saw the heavens torn apart

and the Spirit descending like a dove on him.
And a voice came from heaven,
"You are my Son, the Beloved;
with you I am well pleased."

Mark 1.9-11

Or:

Other Passages (from the liturgy of confirmation):

Isaiah	11.1-4 *on him the Spirit of the Lord rests;* or 42.1-3 *I have endowed my servant with my Spirit;* or 61.1-3, 6, 8-9 *the Lord God has anointed me and has sent me to bring Good News to the poor, to give them the oil of gladness;*
Ezekiel	36.24-28 *I will place a new Spirit in your midst;*
Joel	2.23, 3.1-3 *I will pour out my Spirit on all people;*
Acts	1.3-8 *you will receive the power of the Holy Spirit, and you will be my witnesses;* or 2.1-6, 14, 22-23, 32-33 *they were all filled with the Holy Spirit, and began to speak;* or 8.1, 4, 14-17 *they laid hands on them, and they received the Holy Spirit;* or 10.1, 33-34, 37-44 *the Holy Spirit came down on all those listening to the word of God;* or 19.1-6 *did you receive the Holy Spirit when you became believers?*
Romans	5.1-2, 5-8 *the love of God has been poured into our hearts by the Holy Spirit which has been given to us;* or 8.26-27 *the Spirit himself will express our plea in a way that could never be put into words;*
1 Corinthians	12.4-13 *there is one and the same Spirit given to each as he wills;*
Galatians	5.16-17, 22-23, 24-25 *if we live in the Spirit, let us be directed by the Spirit;*
Ephesians	1.3, 4,13-19 *you have been signed with the seal of the Holy Spirit of the promise;* or 4.1-6 *there is one body, one Spirit, and one baptism;*
Matthew	5.1-12 *theirs is the kingdom of heaven;* or 16.24-27 *if anyone wishes to follow me, let him deny himself;* or 25.14-30 *because you have been faithful in small matters, come into the joy of your master;*
Luke	4.16-22 *the Spirit of the Lord is upon me;* or 8.4-10, 11-15 *some seed fell into rich soil – these are the people who receive the word and bear fruit in patience;* or 10.21-24 *I bless you, Father, for revealing these things to children;*
John	7.37-39 *from the heart of the Lord shall flow fountains of living water;* 14.15-17 *the Spirit of truth will be with you for ever;* or 14.23-26 *the Holy Spirit will teach you everything;* or 15.18-21, 26-27 *the Spirit of truth who issues from the Father, will be my witness;* or 16.5-7, 12-13 *the Spirit of truth will lead you to complete truth.*

INTERCESSIONS

The leader invites all to join in the intercessions. Some of the following invocations may be used.

Leader: Renew the gifts of your Spirit in our lives.

All: *R.* Lord, send us your Spirit.

Another person may read the invocations.

Reader: Fill us with the joy of the Spirit in serving you. *R.*

Strengthen your love in our hearts. *R.*

Refresh those burdened with the cares of life. *R.*

Bring peace to the world. *R.*

Open our eyes to the wonders of your Spirit. *R.*

Or:

Leader: Enlighten our minds
with the guidance of the Holy Spirit.

All: *R.* Lord, send us your Spirit.

Another person may read the invocations.

Reader: Help us to discern the ways of the Spirit. *R.*

Build up the Church, the Body of Christ. *R.*

Bring the Spirit's peace and unity to your Church. *R.*

Turn us away from sin. *R.*

Use our weakness to reflect your
forgiveness and power. *R.*

Or:

Leader: Lord, you bless us with the gift of life.

All: *R.* We give you thanks and praise.

Another person may read the invocations. Other gifts may be mentioned in this litany of thanksgiving.

Reader: You give us your Son as our Savior. R.

You teach us his words of life. R.

You make us your holy people. R.

You cleanse us from our sins. R.

You invite us to love you by loving others. R.

You give us talents to use for your glory. R.

You call us to do good works in response
to your gifts. R.

You nourish us with the bread of life. R.

You give us the cup of salvation. R.

You send us your Spirit. R.

You promise us the joys of heaven. R.

You call us to sing your praises for ever. R.

THE LORD'S PRAYER

The leader introduces the Lord's Prayer in these or similar words.

Leader: The Spirit bears witness with our spirit,
now let us offer together the prayer
our Lord Jesus Christ taught us:

All: Our Father....

PRAYER

The leader may conclude with the following prayer.

Leader: Almighty God,
creator of the world and sanctifier of your people,
we praise you for your glory and power,
revealed in your love for all humanity.

➤

We thank you for saving us
through the death and rising of Jesus,
and for making us temples of your Holy Spirit.

As we prepare to celebrate confirmation,
send us the gifts of your Holy Spirit,
strengthen us in your service,
and guide us in the footsteps of Jesus our brother.

Glory and praise to you, Lord of salvation,
through Jesus Christ your Son,
in the love and unity of your Holy Spirit,
now and always and for ever.

All: Amen.

Or:

Leader: All-powerful God, Father of our Lord Jesus Christ,
by water and the Holy Spirit
you free your sons and daughters from sin
and give them new life.

Send your Holy Spirit upon us
to be our helper and guide.
Give us the spirit of wisdom and understanding,
the spirit of right judgment and courage,
the spirit of knowledge and reverence.
Fill us with the spirit of wonder and awe
in your presence.

We ask this through Christ our Lord.

All: Amen.

CONCLUSION

All may exchange a sign of peace.
A concluding song may be sung.

First Eucharist

First Eucharist completes the sacraments of Christian Initiation: baptism, confirmation and Eucharist.

First Communion is celebrated with the parish community on the Lord's Day, usually within the Easter season. The texts of the Sunday Eucharist are used.

In the days before first Communion, the prayers from the Anniversary of Baptism may be used.

The following form may be used in place of mealtime prayers.

Introduction

Leader: How gracious you are, Lord:
your gift of bread from heaven
reveals your love and brings us perfect joy.
You fill the hungry with good things
and send away empty the rich in their pride.

Or:

Leader: How holy this feast
in which Christ is our food:
his passion is recalled,
grace fills our hearts,
and we receive a pledge of the glory to come.

SCRIPTURE READING

One of the following passages may be read.

Leader: Let us listen to these words from Scripture.

Reader: Jesus said to his disciples,
   "Very truly, I tell you,
   unless you eat the flesh of the Son of Man
   and drink his blood, you have no life in you.
   "Those who eat my flesh and drink my blood
   have eternal life,
   and I will raise them up on the last day;
   for my flesh is true food and my blood is true drink.
   "Those who eat my flesh and drink my blood
   abide in me, and I in them."

   John 6.53-56

Or:

Reader: For I received from the Lord
   what I also handed on to you,
   that the Lord Jesus on the night he was betrayed
   took a loaf of bread,
   and when he had given thanks,
   he broke it and said,
   "This is my body that is for you.
   Do this in remembrance of me."

   In the same way
   he took the cup also, after supper, saying,
   "This cup is the new covenant in my blood.
   Do this, as often as you drink it, in remembrance of me."

   For as often as you eat this bread and drink the cup,
   you proclaim the Lord's death until he comes.

   1 Corinthians 11.23-26

Or:

Reader: Jesus said to his disciples,
"I am the bread of life.
Whoever comes to me will never be hungry,
and whoever believes in me will never be thirsty."

John 6.35

RESPONSE

Leader: We are faithful, Lord, to your command:

All: When we eat this bread and drink this cup,
we proclaim your death, Lord Jesus,
until you come in glory.

Or:

Leader: Christ is Lord of all ages!

All: Lord, by your cross and resurrection,
you have set us free.
You are the savior of the world.

Or:

Leader: Praise to you, Lord Jesus,
firstborn from the dead.

All: Dying you destroyed our death,
rising you restored our life.
Lord Jesus, come in glory.

CONCLUSION

All may recite the Lord's Prayer and exchange a sign of peace.

Blessing God in Daily Life

DURING THE DAY

MORNING PRAYERS

CANTICLE OF ZECHARIAH (BENEDICTUS)

Blessed be the Lord, the God of Israel;
he has come to his people and set them free.

He has raised up for us a mighty savior,
born of the house of his servant David.

Through his holy prophets he promised of old,
that he would save us from our enemies,
from the hands of all that hate us.

He promised to show mercy to our fathers
and to remember his holy covenant.

This was the oath he swore to our father Abraham:
to set us free from the hands of our enemies,
free to worship him without fear,
holy and righteous in his sight,
all the days of our life.

You, my child,
shall be called the prophet of the Most High;
for you will go before the Lord to prepare his way,
to give his people knowledge of salvation
by the forgiveness of all their sins.

In the tender compassion of our God
the dawn from on high shall break upon us,
to shine on those who dwell in darkness and the shadow of death,
and to guide our feet into the way of peace. Glory....

Luke 1.68-79, Version of the *Liturgy of the Hours*

For a sung version, see *CBW III*, nos. 13E or 660.

AT THE START OF DAY

This is the day that the Lord has made;
let us rejoice and be glad.

cf. *Psalm* 118.24

Or:

This is another day, O Lord.
I know not what it will bring forth,
but make me ready, Lord,
for whatever it may be.
If I am to stand up, help me to stand bravely.
If I am to sit still, help me to sit quietly.
If I am to lie low, help me to do it patiently.
And if I am to do nothing, let me do it gallantly.
Make these words more than words,
and give me the Spirit of Jesus. Amen.

I CRY TO YOU

O God, early in the morning I cry to you.
Help me to pray
And to concentrate my thoughts on you:
I cannot do this alone.
In me there is darkness,
But with you there is light;
I am lonely, but you do not leave me;
I am feeble in heart, but with you there is help;
I am restless, but with you there is peace.
In me there is bitterness, but with you there is patience;
I do not understand your ways,
But you know the way for me
Restore me to liberty,
And enable me to live now
That I may answer before you and before me.
Lord, whatever this day may bring,
Your name be praised.

Dietrich Bonhoeffer

A Child's Prayer for Morning

Suitable for children under the age of seven.

Now, before I run to play,
Let me not forget to pray
To God who kept me through the night
And waked me with the morning light.

Help me, Lord, to love thee more
Than I ever loved before,
In my work and in my play
Be thou with me through the day. Amen.

Traditional

Evening Prayers

Canticle of Mary (Magnificat)

My soul proclaims the greatness of the Lord,
my spirit rejoices in God my Savior,
for he has looked with favor on his lowly servant.

From this day all generations will call me blessed:
the Almighty has done great things for me,
and holy is his Name.

He has mercy on those who fear him
in every generation.

He has shown the strength of his arm,
he has scattered the proud in their conceit.

He has cast down the mighty from their thrones,
and has lifted up the lowly.

He has filled the hungry with good things,
and the rich he has sent away empty.

He has come to the help of his servant Israel
for he has remembered his promise of mercy,
the promise he made to our fathers,
to Abraham and his children for ever. Glory....

Luke 1.46-55, Version of the *Liturgy of the Hours*

For a sung version, see *CBW III*, nos. 141 or 674-678.

Praise at Sundown

O gracious light,
pure brightness of the ever–living Father in heaven,
O Jesus Christ, holy and blessed!

Now as we come to the setting of the sun,
and our eyes behold the vesper light,
we sing your praised, O God:
Father, Son, and Holy Spirit.

You are worthy at all times to be praised
by happy voices,
O Son of God, O Giver of Life,
and to be glorified through all the worlds.

An Evening Family Prayer

Lord, behold our family here assembled.
We thank you for this place in which we dwell;
for the love that unites us;
for the peace accorded to us this day;
for the hope with which we expect the morrow;
for the health, the work, the food and the bright skies
that make our lives delightful;
for our friends in all parts of the earth. Amen.

Robert Louis Stevenson

Abide with us, O Lord,
for it is toward evening and the day is far spent;
abide with us, and with thy whole Church.
Abide with us in the evening of the day,
in the evening of life,
in the evening of the world.
Abide with us and with all thy faithful ones,
O Lord, in time and eternity. Amen.

Or:

Almighty God,
we give you thanks for surrounding us,
as daylight fades,
with the brightness of the vesper light;
and we implore you of your great mercy that,
as you enfold us with the radiance of this light,
so you would shine into our hearts
the brightness of your Holy Spirit;
through Jesus Christ our Lord. Amen.

Or:

Grant us, Lord, the lamp of charity which never fails,
that it may burn in us
and shed its light on those around us,
and that by its brightness
we may have a vision of that holy City,
where dwells the true and never-failing Light,
Jesus Christ our Lord. Amen.

Or:

O Lord God Almighty,
as you have taught us to call the evening,
the morning, and the noonday one day;
and have made the sun to know its going down:
Dispel the darkness of our hearts,
that by your brightness
we may know you to be the true God and eternal light,
living and reigning for ever and ever. Amen.

Or:

Seek him who made the Pleiades and Orion,
and turns deep darkness into the morning,
and darkens the day into night;
who calls for the waters of the sea
and pours them out upon the surface of the earth:
The Lord is his name.

Amos 5.8

Or:

Lord Jesus, stay with us,
for evening is at hand and the day is past;
be our companion on the way,
kindle our hearts,
and awaken hope,
that we may know you
as you are revealed in Scripture
and the breaking of bread.
Grant this for the sake of your love. Amen.

A CHILD'S EVENING HYMN

Suitable for children under the age of seven.

I hear no voice, I feel no touch,
I see no glory bright;
But yet I know that God is near,
In darkness as in light.

He watches ever by my side,
And hears my whispered prayer:
The Father for His little child
Both night and day doth care.

Anonymous

NIGHT PRAYERS

CANTICLE OF SIMEON (NUNC DIMITTIS)

Ant.   Protect us, Lord, as we stay awake;
watch over us as we sleep,
that awake, we may keep watch with Christ,
and asleep, rest in his peace.

V.   Lord, now you let your servant go in peace;
your word has been fulfilled:
my own eyes have seen the salvation,
which you have prepared in the sight of every people:
a light to reveal you to the nations
and the glory of your people Israel. Glory....

Luke 2.29-32, Version of the *Liturgy of the Hours.*

BLESS THE LORD

Behold now, bless the Lord,
all you servants of the Lord,
you that stand by night in the house of the Lord.

Lift up your hands in the holy place
and bless the Lord;
the Lord who made heaven and earth
bless you out of Zion.

See *Psalm* 134

A Prayer for Sleep

O heavenly Father,
you give your children sleep
for the refreshing of soul and body:
Grant me this gift, I pray;
keep me in that perfect peace
which you have promised
to those whose minds are fixed on you;
and give me such a sense of your presence,
that in the hours of silence
I may enjoy the blessed assurance of your love;
through Jesus Christ our Lord. Amen.

Or:

My God, I love you with all my heart.
I thank you for having kept me safe this day.
Pardon me the evil I have done,
and accept the good I have done.
Take care of me while I sleep
and deliver me from all danger.
May your grace be always with me
and with all my loved ones. Amen.

Or:

O Lord, support us all the day long,
until the shadows lengthen
and the evening comes,
and the busy world lies hushed,
and the fever of life is over,
and our work is done.
Then in your mercy
grant us a safe lodging,
and a holy rest,
and peace at the last. Amen.

A Child's Bedtime Prayer

Suitable for children under the age of seven.

Angels bless and angels keep
Angels guard me while I sleep
Bless my heart and bless my home
Bless my spirit as I roam
Guide and guard me through the night
and wake me with the morning's light. Amen.

Or:

Now I lay me down to sleep,
I pray Thee, Lord, thy child to keep:
Thy love guard me through the night
And wake me with the morning light. Amen.

Traditional

Or:

Loving Father, put away
All the wrong I've done today;
Make me sorry, true, and good;
Make me love thee as I should;
Make me feel by day and night
I am ever in thy sight.
Heavenly Father, hear my prayer,
Take thy child into thy care;
Let thy angels pure and bright
Watch around me through the night. Amen.

Or the prayer *Angel of God*, page 289.

BLESSING GOD AT MEAL TIME

Meals are special times when members of a family or community have the opportunity to gather and pray. Whatever we eat or drink, or whatever we do, Saint Paul tells us to do it in the name of Christ Jesus for the glory of God. (*1 Corinthians* 10.31)

The Christian Church continues the Jewish tradition of praising God over the food we eat. Any customary form of prayer or grace may be said before and after meals, or one of the following. A litany in keeping with the liturgical season or a general prayer of praise or of thanks may also be appropriate on some occasions.

Festive meals are an image and foretaste of the heavenly banquet. Any meal among friends and relatives may be a reminder that we are brothers and sisters in Christ, who often described the kingdom of heaven as a banquet prepared by his Father. These meals may also remind us of the Eucharistic banquet celebrated each week in our community on the Lord's Day.

This time of prayer may be composed of different elements: a short scripture reading, a psalm or prayer of praise, and intercessions. Litanies, intercessions, and prayers may be chosen from the appropriate section for each liturgical season. Prayers may also reflect the time of day.

The following prayers may be adapted for personal use, or for family or larger gatherings, as needed. The two proposed forms, *Before Meals* and *After Meals,* may be used in the same meal. If it is more convenient, one of the two could be used.

Before Meals

Introduction

When the members of the family have gathered around the table, all make the sign of the cross as the leader begins:

Leader: In the name of the Father, and of the Son, ✠ and of the Holy Spirit.

All: Amen.

Scripture Reading

The gospel of the day may be read, especially on Sunday.
The following texts may also be used.

Leader: Let us listen to these words from Scripture.

Reader: If you offer your food to the hungry
and satisfy the needs of the afflicted,
then your light shall rise in the darkness
and your gloom be like the noonday.

Isaiah 58.10

Or:

Reader: O Lord, how manifold are your works!
In wisdom you have made them all;
the earth is full of your creatures.
These all look to you
to give them their food in due season;
when you give it to them, they gather it up;
when you open your hand,
they are filled with good things.

Psalm 104.24, 27-28

Or:

Reader: Do not be afraid, little flock,
for it is your Father's good pleasure
to give you the kingdom.
Sell your possessions, and give alms.
Make purses for yourselves that do not wear out,
an unfailing treasure in heaven,
where no thief comes near and no moth destroys.
For where your treasure is,
there your heart will be also.

Luke 12.32-34

Or:

Other Passages:

Isaiah   58.1-9 *a fasting pleasing to God;* or 58.9b-14 *the Lord will satisfy your needs;*

Matthew   6.1-4 *whenever you give alms;* or 6.16-18 *fasting in secret;* or 6.19-21 *true treasure;* or 6.24-34 *trust in providence;* or 9.14-15 *a discussion on fasting;* or 25.31-46 *I was hungry and you gave me food;*

Luke   12.35-40 *on being ready for the Master's return.*

On a day of fasting or abstinence, one of the following may be read:

Reader: Is not this the fast that I choose:
to loose the bonds of injustice,
to undo the thongs of the yoke,
to let the oppressed go free,
and to break every yoke?
Is it not to share your bread with the hungry,
and bring the homeless poor into your house;
when you see the naked, to cover them,
and not hide yourself from your own kin?

Isaiah 58.6-7

Or:

Reader: If a brother or sister is naked and lacks daily food,
and one of you says to them,
"Go in peace; keep warm, and eat your fill,"
and yet you do not supply their bodily needs,
what is the good of that?

James 2.15-16

On a day of penance one of the penitential psalms may be prayed: *Psalm 6, 32, 38, 51, 102, 130,* or *145.*

Reader: Out of the depths I cry to you, O Lord.
Lord hear my voice!
Let your ears be attentive
to the voice of my supplications.

If you, O Lord, should mark iniquities,
Lord, who could stand?
But there is forgiveness with you,
so that you may be revered.

I wait for the Lord, my soul waits,
and in his word I hope;
my soul waits for the Lord
more than those who watch for the morning.

O Israel, hope in the Lord!
For with the Lord there is steadfast love,
and with him is great power to redeem.
It is he who will redeem Israel from all its iniquities.

Psalm 130

INTERCESSIONS

The members of the family may speak their intentions at this time.
All respond with silent prayer or a verbal response, such as "Lord, hear our prayer."
A litany in keeping with the liturgical season may also be prayed.

THE LORD'S PRAYER

It is suitable for the leader to invite all to recite the Lord's Prayer by saying:

Leader: We pray with Jesus, our brother:

All: Our Father....

Prayer of Praise

One of the following prayers may be used alone or to conclude the intercessions.

Leader: Blessed are you, Lord God of all creation,
through your goodness we have this food to eat
and family and friends to share it.
May it be for us a sign of your heavenly banquet.

All: Blessed be God for ever.

Or:

Leader: Blessed are you, Lord God of all creation:
you bring forth bread from the earth
to nourish body and spirit
and wine to gladden our hearts.
May the companionship we enjoy at this table
be a pledge of the eternal banquet.

All: Blessed be God for ever.

Or:

Leader: Loving God,
we praise and bless you
for bringing us together for this meal:
may we continue to live in your friendship
and in harmony with each other.
Bless this food, a sign of your loving care for us,
and give us each day our daily bread.
Look with favor
on your Church throughout the world
and on all who seek to do your will today.

We ask this through Jesus Christ our Lord.

All: Amen.

Or:

Leader: Bless us, O Lord,
and these your gifts,
which you have given us in your goodness
through Jesus Christ our Lord.

All: Amen.

Or:

Leader: Bless us, O Lord,
and these your gifts,
which we are about to receive
from your bounty.
Through Christ our Lord.

All: Amen.

On Sunday or a Feast Day

Leader: Blessed are you, Lord God of all creation:
you raised your beloved Son from the dead,
and made him Lord of all people.
We turn to you in prayer
and ask you to bless us and this food,
which in your goodness you have given us.

Help us to be generous toward others,
and to work with them
so that all people may eat well.
Loving God,
grant that as we gather around this table,
so one day we may all celebrate together
around your table in heaven.

We praise you and give you glory
through Jesus Christ our Lord.

All: Amen.

On Friday

Leader: Lord God,
we praise and bless you for having saved us
through the suffering and death of Jesus your Son.
Forgive us our sins and lead us to greater dedication:
teach us to be obedient in faith,
always ready to serve you by our love for others.
Bless this food, and make us truly grateful
for all the gifts you have shared with us
through Jesus Christ our Lord.

All: Amen.

On a Penitential Day

A meal during Lent or on another day of penance may be the occasion for the
family to gather an offering for the poor. When there is no offering, the words
in parenthesis are omitted.

Leader: Bless this food, Lord,
which you have given us in your mercy:
may it refresh our spirits,
bring us strength to work in your service,
and renew our gratitude for your loving care.
(Look with favor on this offering of our love
and accept it as a token of thanksgiving
in return for your many gifts.)
Open our hearts to the blessings
promised to the poor in spirit
that we may always trust in your providence.

We offer you glory and honor and praise
through Jesus Christ, our Savior and Lord,
who lives and reigns for ever and ever.

All: Amen.

On a Special Occasion

Leader: Father,
we praise you for salvation in Jesus, our brother,
and for the action of the Holy Spirit
who binds us together.
Be with us today and grace our gathering.
Bless this meal that we share,
protect us always and make us grow in your love.

Merciful God, we praise your holy Name
now and for ever.

All: Amen.

A Child's Grace

Suitable for children under the age of seven.

Child: God is great and God is good,
And we thank him for our food;
By his hand we must be fed,
Give us Lord, our daily bread.

All: Amen.

Traditional

Seasonal Prayers

Advent, pages 216-222. Christmas, pages 235-242. Lent, pages 250-258.
Holy Week, pages 261-264. Easter, pages 271-276.

AFTER MEALS

RESPONSORY

Leader: By this everyone will know that you are my disciples.

All: If you have love for one another.

Or:

Leader: How very good and pleasant it is.

All: When kindred live together in unity!

Or:

Leader: Blessed be the name of the Lord.

All: Now and for ever.

Or:

Leader: Sing to the Lord, bless his name.

All: Tell of his salvation from day to day.

Or:

Leader: The Lord is merciful and gracious.

All: Slow to anger and abounding in steadfast love.

Or:

Leader: You shall love the Lord your God with all your heart, and with all your soul, and with all your mind.

All: You shall love your neighbor as yourself.

Concluding Prayer

Special forms may be developed.

Leader: Father of mercy,
we give you praise and glory
for the wonderful gifts you have given us:
for life and health, for faith and love,
and for this meal we have shared together.

We thank you, O God,
through Jesus Christ our Lord.

All: Amen.

Or:

Leader: Lord God,
for our food we thank you,
for our joys we praise you,
for our life we glorify you.
Help us to love you more.

All: Amen.

Or:

Leader: Thank you, Lord, for your gifts:
help us to love you more.

All: Amen.

Or:

Leader: We give you thanks for all your benefits,
almighty God,
who live and reign for ever.
May the souls of the faithful departed
through the mercy of God
rest in peace.

All: Amen.

During the Year

MOTHER'S DAY (Second Sunday in May)

Leader: Holy God,
you compared your own love for your people
to the love of a mother for her children.
Look with kindness on our mother
who has shared in your creating love
by the gift of her children.

We thank you for the joys and sorrows of her life,
the giving and sharing,
and, especially for your love
that has formed us in your image.

Listen to our prayers
and bless the mother
who has nurtured and sustained us.
Give her patience in abundance
and let her find joy and satisfaction in all her work.

Glory and praise to you, loving God,
through Jesus Christ our Lord,
who was born of the Virgin Mary,
and who reigns with you in the glory of heaven,
for ever and ever.

All: Amen.

FATHER'S DAY (Third Sunday in June)

Leader: God our Father,
we praise you and bless you
for the life you have given us
through your saving love,
revealed in Jesus your Son.
Through Christ you have revealed yourself
as a loving father who provides for us all.

Look with love upon our father
and bless him with your love.
Deepen his love for his wife and family
and make us one in love
with all your holy people
as we proclaim your mighty deeds
and sing your praises.

We offer you praise and glory,
through Jesus Christ our Lord.

All: Amen.

INDEPENDENCE DAY (July 4)

Leader: Lord Jesus,
bring peace to the world.

All: R. Lord, give us your peace.

Leader: Help all nations to work in harmony. R.

Bless our country,
and help us to work together for peace. R.

Guide those who govern us,
and help them to work for the good of all. R.

Make us generous in sharing our gifts
with other people. R.

Teach us to do your will
and to grow in our service to others. *R.*

Lord Jesus Christ,
look on the people of our land
and bless us all.
Help us to be brothers and sisters to all the world
and to work for peace and love.

Be with us, Jesus, and bless our country,
for you are our Lord and Savior for ever.

All: Amen.

THANKSGIVING DAY   (Fourth Thursday in November)*

Leader: Let us listen to these words of Scripture.

Reader: Rejoice in the Lord always;
again I will say, Rejoice.
Let your gentleness be known to everyone.
The Lord is near.
Do not worry about anything,
but in everything by prayer
and supplication with thanksgiving
let your requests be made known to God.
And the peace of God,
which surpasses all understanding,
will guard your hearts
and your minds in Christ Jesus.

Philippians 4.4-7

Or:

---

* In Canada, second Monday in October.

Reader: And let the peace of Christ rule in your hearts,
to which indeed you were called in the one body.
And be thankful.
Let the word of Christ dwell in you richly;
teach and admonish one another in all wisdom;
and with gratitude in your hearts sing psalms,
hymns, and spiritual songs to God.
And whatever you do, in word or deed,
do everything in the name of the Lord Jesus,
giving thanks to God the Father through him.

Colossians 3.15-17

Or:

Reader: But we appeal to you, brothers and sisters,
to respect those who labor among you,
and have charge of you in the Lord and admonish you;
esteem them very highly in love because of their work.
Be at peace among yourselves.
And we urge you, beloved, to admonish the idlers,
encourage the fainthearted, help the weak,
be patient with all of them.
See that none of you repays evil for evil,
but always seek to do good to one another and to all.

Rejoice always,
pray without ceasing,
give thanks in all circumstances;
for this is the will of God in Christ Jesus for you.
Do not quench the Spirit.
Do not despise the words of prophets,
but test everything; hold fast to what is good;
abstain from every form of evil.

May the God of peace himself sanctify you entirely;
and may your spirit and soul and body
be kept sound and blameless
at the coming of our Lord Jesus Christ.
The one who calls you is faithful, and he will do this.

1 Thessalonians 5.12-24

Leader: Generous God, you bless us with the gift of life.

All: R. We give you thanks and praise.

Leader: You give us your Son as our Savior. R.

You teach us his words of life. R.

You make us your holy people. R.

You cleanse us from our sins. R.

You invite us to love you by loving others. R.

You give us talents to use for your glory. R.

You help us to do good works. R.

You nourish us with the bread of life. R.

You give us the cup of salvation. R.

You send us the gift of your Spirit. R.

You promise us the joys of heaven. R.

You call us to sing your praises. R.

Loving God,
you have given us grace and life
through the hands of Christ our Savior.
With Jesus, we bless your name.
With him, we thank you and pray:

All: Our Father....

Leader: For the kingdom, the power, and the glory are yours,
now and for ever.

Thanksgiving for the Harvest, page 125.

Veterans Day (November 11)

Leader: Loving God,
    have mercy on your people,
    and open our hearts to peace and love.
    Reward all who have died for their country,
    and grant that all nations
    may continue to work for peace and justice.

    Bless us in your service,
    and help us to follow Jesus Christ,
    who is our Savior and our Lord
    for ever and ever.

All: Amen.

Or:

Leader: Blessed are those who have died in the Lord;
    let them rest from their labors
    for their good deeds go with them.
    Eternal rest grant unto them, O Lord.

All: And let perpetual light shine upon them.

Leader: May they rest in peace.

All: Amen.

Or:

Leader: We bow our heads in prayer,
    and pray to God for peace.

All pause for a moment of silent prayer.

Leader: Father of our Lord Jesus Christ,
    have mercy on all the world.
    Pour the Spirit of peace into the hearts of all,
    and help us to be peacemakers
    who work for harmony and love.
    Grant this through Christ our Lord.

All: Amen.

AT SCHOOL

At the Beginning of a School Year / Semester / Term

Leader: Blessed are you, Lord God,
creator of body and mind and heart;
you have sent the Spirit of wisdom and knowledge
to guide your people in all their ways.

At the beginning of this new school year (semester/term),
we implore your mercy:
bless the students, teachers and staff of N.,
that together we may grow in faith, hope, and love
as we learn from you and each other
how to follow your Son, Jesus.

Expand the horizons of our minds,
that we may grow in wisdom,
understanding and knowledge;
deepen our commitment to seek the truth of your ways;
and enliven our faith to reach out to those in need.

Glory and praise to you, Lord God,
in the Church and in Christ Jesus for ever and ever.

All: Amen.

Or:

Leader: God of wisdom and might,
we praise you for the wonders of our being,
for mind, body, and spirit.
Be with our children as they begin
a new school year (semester/term).
Bless them and their teachers and staff.

Give them strength and grace as their bodies grow;
wisdom and knowledge to their minds
as they search for understanding;
and peace and zeal to their spirits.

We ask this through Jesus Christ our Lord.

All: Amen.

At the End of a School Year / Semester / Term

Leader: God of wisdom,
we thank you for all the gifts you have given us
throughout this school year (semester/term).
We praise you for giving us life,
for saving us in Christ,
and for choosing us to be your people.

As we come to the end of this school
year (semester/term),
we voice our gratitude
for the good things you have done in us,
and we praise you for all who have shared
in the work of this school.

We ask you to bless them in your love
and give them refreshment and peace.

We praise you, God,
through Jesus Christ, our Lord,
who lives and reigns for ever and ever.

All: Amen.

FOR A GRADUATION

Leader: Blessed are you, Lord our God,
for you begin all things and bring them to conclusion.
At the dawn of creation you created all things
and placed this earth under our care;
You sent your Son, Jesus
to be the way, the truth, and the life;
and through the gift of the Holy Spirit
guide our way to the glory of your kingdom.

We praise you for our son/daughter:
you have guided him/her to this proud moment.
As we celebrate his/her graduation,
we ask you to continue your gracious guidance
in his/her life.

Open new doors and lead him/her
to marvel at the wonders of creation and life.
May your Spirit help him/her to see
his/her many gifts,
and teach him/her how to share these
in your Church and for the benefit of others.

Continue to bless our family and our children,
and grant that we
may always rejoice in your gift of love.

We ask this through Jesus Christ our Lord,
in the unity of the Holy Spirit,
one God, for ever and ever.

All: Amen.

AT WORK

Blessing Those Seeking Employment

Leader: Loving God,
you created the human race
and you know each one of us by name.
Through Christ you have chosen us
to be your sons and daughters
and to build up your kingdom on earth.

Give N. the work he/she seeks
so that he/she may share his/her talents with others
and know the dignity and satisfaction
that you give us through our work.
Give him/her patience while you open doors
and grant him/her the wisdom to see your will.

Keep our family in your care
and provide for all our needs.
Never let stress diminish our love for each other
nor the desire for material things
lessen our love for you.

With confidence and trust, loving God,
we make this prayer through Jesus Christ our Lord.

All: Amen.

Prayer of Workers

Leader: Blessed are you, Lord God,
from eternity you have called us to be your people,
and to sing your praises at all times.

Bless us in our work and prayer,
and grant that our lives may give you glory
through our words, our witness, and our worship.

We give you praise, creator God,
through Jesus Christ our Lord,
in the communion of the Holy Spirit,
one God, for ever and ever.

All: Amen.

Or:

Leader: Almighty God,
bless me abundantly
and help me in my work;
be with me in all that I do;
keep me from all evil and harm.

See *1 Chronicles* 4.10

MEETING

BEFORE A MEETING

Leader: Blessed are you, bounteous God,
maker of heaven and earth,
you have chosen us to be your people
and to give you glory in everything we do.
Be with us during our meeting,
which will bring many people together.
Help us to meet one another in joy
and to work together for your glory
and the benefit of our community.

We praise your name for ever and ever.

All: Amen.

During a Meeting

Leader: Let us pause to ask God for help.

All pause for a moment of silent prayer.

Leader: Almighty God,
bless us as we gather today for this meeting.
Guide our minds and hearts
so that we will work for the good of our community
and be a help to all people.
Teach us to be generous in our outlook,
courageous in face of difficulty,
and wise in our decisions.

We give you praise and glory, Lord our God,
for ever and ever.

All: Amen.

Or:

Leader: Praise to you, Lord God, of all creation:
you have made the world for us to live in.
Grant us light to know the needs of our community,
and the strength to make wise decisions
for the benefit of all.
Do not let self-interest or greed influence us,
for you have chosen us to serve your people.

Glory be to you for ever and ever.

All: Amen.

At the End of a Meeting

Leader: Father of us all,
look upon us in your love, and bless us.
Protect us from sin and harm,
and guide us with your light
until we come together again.

All praise, glory, and honor to you, Father,
through Christ our Lord.

All: Amen.

BEFORE A BUSINESS TRIP

Leader: Blessed are you, Lord God,
Creator of heaven and earth:
you have given us Jesus as the way,
the truth and the life.
Guide us on our way:
protect us as we travel,
and allow us to arrive home safely.
Give us peace and tranquillity in our journey
and keep our loved ones in your loving embrace.

Glory and praise to you, almighty God,
for ever and ever.

All: Amen.

IN INDUSTRY

BLESSING OF WORKERS

Leader: Blessed are you, Lord our God,
Creator of the universe and Father of humanity.
We praise you for your mighty works
and for the wonders of your love.

Hear our prayers today
and grant your blessings to all workers.
Let our work contribute to the good
of all members of this community
and to your glory for ever and ever.

All: Amen.

BLESSING OUR WORK

Leader: Lord Jesus, bless us this day
and all the work we do.

Help us to share more fully
the resources of your world
for the well-being of all people.
Give us satisfaction in our work
and help us to act with justice and love.
Accept our work and offer it to the Father
as a sacrifice of praise.

We thank you for your Holy Spirit
who teaches us how to pray
and who inspires us to give you glory and praise
for ever and ever.

All: Amen.

BLESSING MACHINERY OR COMPUTERS

Leader: God our Creator, maker of all things,
you have given us the wisdom and talent
to design and build machines/computers.

Help us to use this machinery/computer in our work.
May our work bring you greater glory
and our efforts build up your kingdom on earth.

Holy God, we make this prayer
through Jesus Christ our Lord.

All: Amen.

BLESSING TOOLS AND MACHINERY

Leader: Gracious God,
we praise you for the works of creation
and we ask you to guide us in our work.

Let us use these tools (machinery) in safety
and make us productive in all we do.
Bless those who use them
and let us work for the good of others.

We praise you for all the skills
you have shared with your people,
and we ask that they will always be exercised
for your honor and glory, now and for ever.

All: Amen.

IN THE ARTS

Blessing Artists, Authors, Composers

Leader: Loving God,
you made all things through your Word,
and ordered them
through the outpouring of the Holy Spirit.
You rejoiced at the beauty and goodness
of all that you created,
a beauty that brings joy and happiness
to all your creatures on earth.

Listen to our prayer for artists, authors, and composers:
continue to inspire them by the gifts of the Spirit
that they may interpret for us the meaning of life,
unlock the mysteries of love,
and reveal the depths of goodness
which reflect your presence in creation.

Grant that their work may inspire and uplift all people
as well as challenge us to see
the true value and dignity of life.

Glory and praise to you, God of beauty and love,
through Jesus Christ our Lord.

All: Amen.

In Thanksgiving for a Work of Art

Leader: God our creator,
the heavens declare your glory,
and earth proclaims your handiwork.
We praise you for the work of creation,
manifest in the imagination and skill
of artists and crafts people
who bring beauty and delight,
challenge and vision to our lives.

May your blessing be upon all who share this work:
may we all become heralds of your reign
when beauty shall be the companion
of justice and peace.

We ask this through Christ our Lord.

All: Amen.

ON THE SEA

BLESSING OF A SHIP OR BOAT

Leader: Blessed are you, Lord our God,
         Creator of the universe and Father of all:
         we praise you for your wonderful works,
         and give you glory.

         We thank you for the rivers, lakes, and seas,
         and pray for all who sail upon them.
         Bless this boat (ship) and all who travel in it.

         Protect them afloat and ashore,
         by day and by night,
         and bring us all to peace and security
         with you and all your saints.

         Blessed are you, Lord our God,
         now and always and for ever.

All: Amen.

For the Safety of the Fleet

Leader: Holy Father, Creator of the universe,
you have given the seas and the life they contain
for the use and benefit of all people.

Protect those who set sail during this fishing season,
make them good stewards of this gift,
and give them a bountiful catch.

We ask your help, God of love,
through Jesus Christ our Lord.

All: Amen.

For Protection in Danger

Leader: Lord of all creation,
in you we place our hope
for you hear the cries of those in danger and need.

Protect those at sea from every peril
and bring them safely to port.
Send your Spirit to be with us
to calm every fear,
and make us confident in your loving providence.

We ask this through Jesus Christ our Lord.

All: Amen.

Or:

Leader: Lord Jesus Christ,
as your disciples, caught by a great windstorm,
felt themselves in danger on the sea,
you woke up, rebuked the wind
and said to the sea, "Peace! Be still!"

Watch over those at sea,
keep them from every peril
and bring them safely to port.

Breathe on us,
that your Spirit give us peace,
calm every fear,
and increase our faith in your attentive presence.

You who live and reign with the Father
and the Holy Spirit for ever and ever.

All: Amen.

Blessing of a Fishing Fleet

Leader: Heavenly Father,
you have given your people skills to build boats
in order to harvest the seas.
Bless those who fish, and these boats.
Bring them back to land in safety
with a bountiful catch.
May all who sail the seas
be inspired by your Spirit
to have greater unity with all your creation.

We ask this through Jesus Christ our Lord.

All: Amen.

For a Bountiful Catch

Leader: Eternal God,
Creator of the universe,
you have given the sea and all it contains
for the benefit of your people.

Preserve the gifts you have given.
Protect those who earn their living from the sea.
Provide them with a bountiful catch
and grant that in their work
they may give you praise and glory.

We ask this through Jesus Christ our Lord.

All: Amen.

Leader: Blessed are you, bounteous God,
for we see the marvels of your love
revealed in all creation,
even in the depths of the mighty oceans.

We thank you for your protection upon the sea.
We join our voices to proclaim your greatness
and unite our lives to reflect your goodness.

Glory and praise are yours, Lord God,
for ever and ever.

All: Amen.

IN AGRICULTURE

Farms and Farm Workers

Leader: All praise and glory are yours, Lord our God,
Creator of the universe and Father of all:
we give you thanks for your mercy
and for your loving care of creation.

Continue to shower your blessings on this farm:
on the people who live and work here,
on the animals and plants,
on the buildings and machinery.

Let your people live and work in happiness,
and enjoy the fruits of their labors.
Let the plants and animals flourish,
and be protected from all harm.
Let these buildings and machines
continue to be of service to all.

Almighty God, we bless and glorify your name
now and always and for ever.

All: Amen.

FIELDS AND SEEDS

Leader: Almighty God,
         Lord of creation and giver of life,
         we praise you for your goodness to us.

         At the beginning of the planting season,
         we ask you to give us the weather we need
         to grow our crops,
         and make our fields fertile
         so that they may yield a bountiful harvest.

         Protect all who work here,
         and grant that all our work
         may bring you greater honor and glory
         and lead us closer to you.

         We ask this in the name of Jesus the Lord.

All: Amen.

MEADOWS FOR GRAZING

Leader: Blessed are you, Lord our God,
         maker of the universe and giver of all good gifts:
         we praise you and give you glory
         for the love you show to us.

         Make these fields and meadows fertile,
         and let them provide plentiful food
         for the animals that feed here.
         Grant that the weather may be favorable,
         and our herds and flocks healthy.

         Father, we place ourselves in your hands,
         and give you glory through Jesus Christ our Lord.

All: Amen.

SEED

Leader: Lord God, Creator of heaven and earth,
we bless you and give you glory
for the seed you have given us
and for the mystery of life that it contains.
Bless our planting and make our work fruitful.
Grant that the seeds we plant
will produce plentiful crops,
providing food and work for many.

In your love, give us favorable weather
throughout this growing season.
Make us truly grateful for all our gifts,
and willing to share
our goods and talents with others
especially those without adequate food.

All praise and glory are yours, Lord God,
for ever and ever.

All: Amen.

AGRICULTURAL MACHINERY

Leader: God our Creator,
maker of all things,
you have given us the talent to design machines.
Help us to use this farm machinery in our work.
May we bring you greater glory
by all our actions,
and work to build your kingdom on earth.

Holy God,
we make this prayer through Christ our Lord.

All: Amen.

For the Harvest

Leader: Blessed are you, Lord our God,
Creator of heaven and earth
and Father of our Lord Jesus Christ:
we praise you for your glory
and thank you for your goodness to us.
We praise you for your generous gifts
and for bringing fruitful results to our labors.
As we rejoice in your kindness,
we pray also for those who are in need.
Open our hearts to them,
and teach us to be as generous to others
as you are to us.
Gracious and bounteous God,
help us all to follow Jesus our Lord
and so bear eternal fruit for you.

Blessed are you, Lord our God, for ever and ever.

All: Amen.

FAVORABLE WEATHER

FOR RAIN

Leader: God our Creator,
maker of all things and protector of your people,
in your love look upon us in our time of need
and give us your help.

Open the heavens for us and send us the rain
we need for our lives and crops.
As our hearts long for you,
so we seek rain to refresh the earth;
as we long for life,
so let the earth produce its harvest in abundance.
May we rejoice in the good things of the earth
and raise our eyes to you, the source of all blessings.

Hear our cry for mercy and answer our prayer,
through Jesus Christ our Lord.

All: Amen.

FOR DRY WEATHER

Leader: Almighty God,
look with mercy on us
and swiftly come to our help.
Give us the dry weather we need,
and deliver us from poor crops
(the danger of floods, etc.).
Grant us the good things of the earth
and your spiritual blessings in abundance.

Teach us to be generous to others
and grateful to you for your goodness.

With confidence we make our prayer
though Jesus Christ our Lord.

All: Amen.

For Calm and Moderate Weather

Leader: In your mercy and love, O Lord,
protect your people and come to their aid.
Grant us relief from storms and danger,
and bring us calm and moderate weather.
Let us live secure in your peace,
that we may enjoy the fruits of the earth
and the harvest of your love.
With confidence we make our prayer
though Jesus Christ our Lord.

All: Amen.

For Protection during a Storm

Leader: Loving God, maker of heaven and earth,
protect us in your love and mercy.
Send the Spirit of Jesus to be with us,
to still our fears and give us confidence.
In the stormy waters,
Jesus reassured his disciples by his presence,
calmed the storm, and strengthened their faith.
Guard us from harm during this storm
and renew our faith to serve you faithfully.
Give us the courage to face all difficulties
and the wisdom to see the ways
your Spirit binds us together
in mutual assistance.

With confidence we make our prayer
though Jesus Christ our Lord.

All: Amen.

In Thanksgiving for Good Weather

Leader: Loving God,
we thank you for your gifts to us:
for making this wonderful world,
for choosing us to be your holy people,
and for calling us to build up your kingdom on earth.
We thank you for the good weather you have given to us.
Help us to show our thanks
by sharing our lives and our gifts with others.

We give you thanks and praise
through Jesus Christ your Son,
in the love and unity of your Holy Spirit,
one God, for ever and ever.

All: Amen.

In Thanksgiving for a Beautiful Day

Leader: Gracious God,
we praise you and give you glory
for the wonderful things you do for us:
for life and health,
for friends and family,
for this splendid day.
For all this, we pray as Jesus taught us:

All: Our Father....

ANIMALS AND PETS

BLESSING OF PETS

PRAYER

Leader: Blessed are you, almighty God,
Lord of heaven and earth,
out of nothing you created the earth and sky and sea
and made every living creature to inhabit them.

We praise you for all the animals you made:
the creatures that dwell in the waters,
the birds of the air,
and those that walk upon the face of the earth.

We thank you for the joy they bring us,
the responsibility they teach us,
and the contribution they make to our families
and our well-being.

Bless all these (our) pets,
and grant that our care for them
may help us grow in your love.

We praise you and thank you,
through Jesus Christ our Lord.

All: Amen.

A CHILD'S PRAYER

Suitable for children under the age of seven.

Dear Father, hear and bless
Your beasts and singing birds:
And guard with tenderness
Small things that have no words.

Traditional

For Health and Long Life of a Pet

Leader: Creator God,
we thank you for making animals and creatures
as part of your wonderful creation.
Through *N.* our pet you have touched our hearts
with its presence in our family.

Grant that it may help us
to be more loving and considerate.
Help us to respond to its affection
by showing kindness to all living things
and increasing our respect for creation.

Give health and long life to our pet.

We ask this through Jesus Christ our Lord.

All: Amen.

Blessing a Sick Animal (Pet)

Leader: Loving God,
you have created all things for your glory,
and have made us stewards of this world.
We know
that you love all the creatures you have made,
and so we ask you to look with kindness
on this animal (pet)
and restore it to health and strength.

In the midst of sickness
strengthen our faith in your love
that we may believe that you are able
to bring good out of every situation.

We pray with confidence
through Jesus Christ our Lord.

All: Amen.

COMINGS AND GOINGS

BEFORE MOVING

Leader: Almighty God,
you constantly surprise your people
with new beginnings;
yet each beginning means a farewell
to all that is familiar and sure.

Let us rejoice in the blessings of this house
and our friends and neighbors
and never let us forget the good times we had.

Give us the courage and will
to embrace this new beginning
in the life of our family.
Let us be a consolation and strength
to each other as we face the uncertainty of the future;
and give us true friends and good neighbors.
Be with our children as they attend a new school.
Bring growth out of the challenges that lie ahead,
and open our eyes to your presence in others.

May we bless you in good times and in bad,
in sorrows and in joys,
for you are the God who promises that Christ
will always be with us.

We make this prayer in the power of the Holy Spirit,
who inspires us to sing your praises for ever and ever.

All: Amen.

For a blessing of a (new) home, see pages 24-34 and 35-40.

At Retirement

Leader: All praise and glory are yours,
almighty and eternal God.
You created this earth and all it contains
and placed creation within our care
so that by the work of human hands
we might share in your creative power
and build up human society.

Look with kindness
upon *N.*, our coworker,
who has contributed to our community/company
and who is now retiring/has retired.
Allow him/her the time
to survey all that he/she has accomplished
and give him/her satisfaction and fulfillment
for all his/her labors,
as you did on the seventh day,
when you rested and saw that all you had made was good.

Give him/her peace and help him/her
in this period of adjustment.
Reassure him/her of your love
and open new ways for him/her
to share his/her gifts for the benefit of others.

We praise you, God of love,
through Jesus Christ our Lord.

All: Amen.

Before Leaving Home

Leader: Blessed are you, Lord our God,
for you bless our coming and our going.
Look upon *N.* as he/she leaves home
for new endeavors.
We thank you for the good times we have enjoyed,
the memories that bind us,
and the love that forms us as your people.
We praise you for the dreams and hopes
that lie before *N.*,
and the new challenges that face him/her.
Comfort us who remain with the knowledge
that your love will protect and guard him/her
in the days that lie ahead.
May your peace go with him/her.

We ask this through Jesus Christ our Lord.

All: Amen.

At a Family Celebration or Reunion

Leader: Lord Jesus Christ,
you are the presence of God on earth
and the revelation of his love.
You welcomed all people who came to you
and joined in the festivities of their meals.
Be with us and bless our family gathering
with your presence.
Keep us always in your love
and grant us the joy of celebrating
the mystery of your love in one another.
Bless our time together
(and make us thankful for the food we share).

Accept our prayer, Jesus.
You live and reign for ever and ever.

All: Amen.

Before a Vacation or Trip

Leader: Almighty God, Lord of heaven and earth,
we praise you for the vastness of the earth
and the variety of its formation.

Throughout our vacation (trip)
open our eyes to its beauty,
so that we may discover the wisdom and love
of the One who created it.

Bless our time together,
keep us safe from all harm,
and refresh us in body and spirit.
Be with us through the ways of our journey
and guide us safely home by your loving hand.

We make our prayer through Jesus Christ our Lord.

All: Amen.

Before a Pilgrimage

Leader: Lord God,
when you freed your people from slavery,
you journeyed with them,
guiding them by the light of your presence
to the promised land.

Through the waters of baptism
you led us out of the slavery of sin
into the new life of the Spirit.

Let the light of Christ enlighten our path
and his word unlock for us the mystery of your love.

Hear our prayer as we begin this journey of faith.
Open for us the possibilities for growth
that come from human challenges
and the guidance of the Holy Spirit.

Affirm our faith in this time of fellowship,
(penance), and prayer,
and reveal your strength that shines
through our human weakness.

As we begin with your inspiration and grace,
so bring our journey to completion
through our communion in the Holy Spirit.

To you be glory and praise in the Church,
in Christ your Son, and in the Holy Spirit,
God, for ever and ever.

All: Amen.

BEFORE A PENITENTIAL PILGRIMAGE

Leader: Almighty God,
after his baptism
your Son wandered through the desert
for forty days and nights.
He fasted and prayed
and was strengthen by your word.

Be with us on our journey of faith
as we seek anew your mercy and love.
By our walking and praying,
by our fasting and sharing,
may we discover the depth of your love for us
and the joy and peace
you offer the disciples of your Son.

May your Word light up our pathways,
your Spirit animate our faith
and our fellowship deepen our love.

Receive our prayer of praise and adoration,
which we offer through Jesus Christ our Lord,
in the unity of the Holy Spirit, one God,
now and for ever.

All: Amen.

Upon Return From a Trip or Pilgrimage

Leader: Blessed are you, Lord God,
guide and companion of your people.
When Christ journeyed with his disciples
on the road to Emmaus,
he revealed his presence among them,
as he opened the scriptures and broke the bread.

We thank you for Christ's presence
on our journey of faith
and the insights of the Holy Spirit that reveal to us
the wisdom of your ways
and the wonder of our being.
We praise you for the healing presence of your Spirit,
when we share the stories of our lives
and break the bread of life with others.

We thank you for a safe return,
and ask that the journey of faith we began in baptism
and symbolized in our pilgrimage,
may bring us closer to the unity,
peace, and justice of your kingdom,
where you live and reign for ever and ever.

See *Luke* 24.13-35

All: Amen.

Blessing a Family Car, Van or any Vehicle

Leader: We bless you, Lord God,
for your goodness and loving kindness
to all your people.
We thank you
for the work of human hands and minds
that are able to fashion this car (truck, van, etc.)
for our use.

Bless those who will drive it
and their passengers.
Keep them safe
and protect them from all dangers and hazards.
May we use this vehicle with care and prudence,
for the benefit of our family and friends,
and for the good of those in need.

Almighty God, we ask this blessing,
through Jesus Christ our Lord.

All: Amen.

SPECIAL NEEDS AND OCCASIONS

*Each of these prayers is introduced by a petition which may be followed by a period
of silence.*

IN TIMES OF SORROW

Leader: For those who mourn:
Lord, console them in their grief,
and brighten their tomorrows
with the promise of your love.

(We pray for.... Intentions and/or names may be added.)

Blessed are you, Lord our God, ruler of all creation:
we praise you for the many gifts
you have showered on us in your love.
Dry the tears of sorrow
with the consolation of your loving presence.
Help us now in our time of sorrow,
and lift us when we are crushed,
for we entrust our lives into your hands.

We ask this through Jesus Christ our Lord.

All: Amen.

In Times of Crisis

For One Person

Leader: For all people in need, especially *N.*:
Lord, ease all their burdens,
and give them your strength.

(We pray for.... Intentions and/or names may be added.)

Lord Jesus, Prince of Peace,
bring your healing and peace into *N.'s* life.
Show him/her your mercy and love
and uphold him/her in this time of crisis
by sending your Holy Spirit into his/her heart.

Lord Jesus, hear our prayer,
for you are our brother and our Lord.

All: Amen.

All may lay their hands in silent prayer on the person's head.

For a Family or Group or Community

Leader: For our family (friends or community)
in this time of crisis:
Lord, sustain us with your strength
and guide us in the ways of wisdom.

(We pray for.... Intentions and/or names may be added.)

Almighty God,
you are blessed throughout all ages
for your mercy and love.
Look upon us in our time of need
and give us the strength
to persevere in your love.
Protect your people from all harm
and guide us with the light of your face
until we overcome all dangers (setbacks).

We make this prayer through Jesus Christ our Lord.

All: Amen.

In Times of Need

Leader: For those in any need:
almighty God, keep them in your love
and make us generous in responding to those in need.

(We pray for.... Intentions and/or names may be added.)

Lord God,
we turn to you in all our troubles
and praise you in all our joys.

Hear our prayer this day and see our need (*N.*).
Give us the strength and courage
that flows from your Spirit
to follow your Son, Jesus, in the way of the cross.
Send us your support
and let us experience it
in the generosity and support of others.
Glory and praise to you, God of mercy,
through Jesus Christ our Lord.

All: Amen.

IN TIMES OF TROUBLE

Leader: For those in difficulty:
Lord, see our trouble,
and do not let us fall.

(We pray for.... Intentions and/or names may be added.)

For our family in time of uncertainty:
Lord, guard us from all evil,
and be at our right hand.

(We pray for.... Intentions and/or names may be added.)

For those seeking employment:
Lord, remove the clouds that hinder us
from seeing your face,
and keep us on the path of righteousness.

(We pray for.... Intentions and/or names may be added.)

We praise you, Lord God,
for you are strength for the frail,
rest for the weary,
and consolation for the downhearted.
Be our refuge of strength and rock of salvation,
and look upon our troubled spirits.
Give us the peace to trust you
in all things and at all times.

We make our prayer though Jesus Christ our Lord.

All: Amen.

For Help

Leader: For God's help in all our needs:
Lord, give us the strength we require
to live in faith, hope, and love.

(We pray for.... Intentions and/or names may be added.)

Blessed are you, Lord God, our rock and strength:
you have called us to be your people;
you have rescued us from darkness and sin,
and have brought us into your wonderful light.

Help us in our weakness by the power of your Spirit,
and make us channels of your love,
that we may respond to the challenges of life
that are set before us.

Fill our hearts with peace and light,
that we may have the faith
to see your hand at work in the world
and the hope to believe
that you are able to bring good out of every situation.

We give you praise and glory
and raise our prayer to you
through Jesus Christ our Lord.

All: Amen.

FOR FORGIVENESS

Leader: For those who have hurt us;
Lord, heal our hearts with your love,
and give us the strength to forgive them
as you forgive us.

(We pray for.... Intentions and/or names may be added.)

All praise and glory and blessing be to you,
Lord God of mercy:
you have loved us so deeply
that you gave us your only Son, our Savior,
as our peace and reconciliation.

Jesus taught us
that we are all sinners in your sight.
He invites us to forgive those
who have sinned against us
with the same love by which you forgive us.

Heal our wounded hearts that seek revenge,
and transform them
with the light and peace of the Holy Spirit.
We pray for your forgiveness for those
who have injured us:
let us reach out in forgiveness
that we may love others as you love us.

We know that we are weak,
and so we ask you to make us strong
that we may obey your commands
and live in your peace.
God of love, we bless your name
through Jesus Christ your Son,
in the communion of your Spirit,
now and for ever and ever.

All: Amen.

Or:

Leader: Lord Jesus,
we thank you for loving us,
for suffering and dying to save us from sin,
for rising to new life in glory,
and for calling us to share in your life and joy.

Have mercy on us in our weakness.
Give us a generous spirit to forgive our enemies.

Transform our thoughts and desires for retribution
into acts of love and forgiveness.

You are Lord for ever and ever.

All: Amen.

Before An Election

Leader: For those running for public office,
and for all voters:
Lord, give all of us wisdom and discernment.

(We pray for.... Intentions and/or names may be added.)

Loving God,
help the people
of our community (state or country)
to make wise choices in the forthcoming election.

Enlighten us and those who will be elected
with the wisdom and fortitude to do your will.
Strengthen the gifts of your Spirit
so that we may work together
for your glory and the good of all citizens.

We offer this prayer through Jesus Christ our Lord.

All: Amen.

Planning a Special Project

The following prayer may be adapted by adding a description of the project. The second part of the prayer may be used as a blessing at the conclusion of an event or gathering.

Leader: Blessed are you, Lord God,
ruler of all creation:
you know our hearts and our plans,
and guide all that we do for your glory.
Bless us as we continue to do our work
and bless all that we do for you.
Help us to carry out all our activities
for your honor and glory
and for the salvation of your people.
Guide us in all we do;
help us to build up your kingdom
and come to our reward.

We praise your name for ever and ever.

All: Amen.

Or:

Leader: Lord,
direct our actions by your inspiration
and carry them out by your assistance.
May our every prayer and work
always begin with you
and through you come to a successful completion.

All: Amen.

Blessing God at the Time of Sickness

Jesus showed his love for the sick by visiting them, by touching them, by forgiving and healing them. He encourages us to recognize him in our sick brothers and sisters (Matthew 25.31-40). Throughout the centuries, the people of God have continued to express this love and care for those who are sick.

The sick are remembered in the daily prayer of the Church and especially at Eucharist during the Prayer of the Faithful. Communion is brought frequently, even daily, to the sick. The Church's ritual book, *Pastoral Care of the Sick and the Dying*, contains many prayers and blessings for the sick.

Since sickness often provides time and inclination for greater prayer and reflection, these moments should be encouraged. In the room of the sick, it is good to have a Bible, New Testament, or book of psalms; a cross or crucifix and holy pictures or statues. Blessed water may be placed within reach of the sick person.

ANOINTING OF THE SICK

Anointing of the Sick is the Church's sacrament for those who are seriously ill by reason of sickness or age. The parish priest should be invited to celebrate the sacrament of the Anointing of the Sick with the sick and their family, friends, and neighbors. This should take place early on in the illness so that the sick person as well as his/her family may participate in the celebration and derive comfort from it. The anointing may be repeated if the sick person recovers and then falls ill again or if the condition becomes more serious.

When the Anointing of the Sick is celebrated, or when Holy Communion is brought, it is useful to have a table covered with a cloth and with a lighted candle near the bed of the sick person. A glass of water is helpful for the reception of Communion.

If the sick person wishes to go to confession, it is preferable that this take place at an earlier visit. Reconciliation may take place at the beginning of the anointing or before the celebration.

Outline of the Rite of Anointing

Introductory rites

Greeting
Sprinkling with holy water
Instruction
Penitential rite

Liturgy of the Word

Liturgy of Anointing

Litany
Laying on of hands
Prayer over the oil
Anointing
Prayer after anointing
Lord's Prayer

(Holy Communion)

Concluding rite

Blessing

Family and friends are invited and encouraged to take an active part in the celebration of anointing. They are witnesses to the prayerful concern of the entire Church.

> Through this holy anointing
> may the Lord in his love and mercy help you
> with the grace of the Holy Spirit.
>
> May the Lord who frees you from sin
> save you and raise you up.

For the celebration of the Anointing of the Sick, see *Pastoral Care of the Sick: Rites of Anointing and Viaticum* (1983) pages 74-102.

Visits to the Sick, the Homebound and the Elderly

During the years of his ministry, Jesus showed his compassion for the sick on many occasions. He sent his apostles to lay hands on them and anoint them with healing oil (*Mark* 6.13).

The Lord Jesus also reminded us, in speaking of the day of judgement, that we visit him when we visit the sick, and reject him when we refuse to come to their aid (*Matthew* 25.31-46).

Introduction

The visitors greet the person informally and, if unknown, introduce themselves. The visitors may then speak quietly with the sick person, and should be comfortable with times of silence as well.

> One of them may begin a time of prayer with the sign of the cross and a greeting. The leader may say:

Leader: Lord, by your cross and resurrection,

All: You have set us free.
You are the Savior of the world.

> Or:

Leader: *N.*, trust the Lord, for God is always with you.

Scripture Reading

One of the following readings may be chosen.

Leader: Let us listen to these words from Scripture.

Reader: When Jesus had come down from the mountain,
great crowds followed him;
and there was a leper who came to him
and knelt before him, saying,
"Lord, if you choose, you can make me clean."
He stretched out his hand and touched him, saying,
"I do choose. Be made clean!"
Immediately his leprosy was cleansed.

Matthew 8.1-3

Or:

Reader: When they got out of the boat,
people at once recognized Jesus,
and rushed about that whole region
and began to bring the sick on mats
to wherever they heard he was.
And wherever he went,
into villages or cities or farms,
they laid the sick in the marketplaces,
and begged him
that they might touch even the fringe of his cloak;
and all who touched it were healed.

Mark 6.54-56

Or:

Other Passages:

Matthew	8.14-17 *a number of cures;*
Luke	5.12-16 *cure of a man suffering from a virulent skin disease;* or 18.35-43 *cure of a blind man in Jericho;*
Acts	3.1-10 *cure of a lame man.*

Or:

A psalm may be prayed:

Reader: O Lord, my heart is not lifted up,
my eyes are not raised too high;
I do not occupy myself with things
too great and too marvellous for me.

But I have calmed and quieted my soul,
like a weaned child with its mother;
my soul is like the weaned child that is within me.

O Israel, hope in the Lord
from this time on and forevermore.

Psalm 131

Also, *Psalm* 8, 23, 27, 100, 102, 117 or another suitable psalm may be selected. The reading may be followed by a moment of silent prayer.

INTERCESSIONS

Other intentions and concerns expressed by the person may be included.

Leader: Let us respond in faith to God's Word
and seek his strength and consolation in Christ.

All: R. Lord, hear our prayer.
or: Lord, hear us.
or: Lord, have mercy.

Another person may read the intentions:

Reader: Lord God,
turn your ear to us, and let our prayer come to you. R.

Mighty Savior,
do not hide your face from those in distress. R.

Divine Healer, strengthen our faith and hope. R.

God most high,
give us a spirit of praise all the days of our life. R.

Lord of heaven and earth,
give us light and salvation. R.

God of mercy, keep us safe from evil and despair. R.

Loving God, be our stronghold in time of trial. R.

God of glory,
let us dwell in your presence for ever. R.

Father of Jesus,
keep us one in the Body of Christ. R.

Or:

Reader: For those confined to their home or hospital,
we pray. R.

For their families and friends and all who support them,
we pray. R.

For those who care for the sick, we pray. R.

For all who have lost hope or their zest for life,
we pray. R.

For young people and parents, we pray. R.

For those who serve Christ in the sick, we pray. R.

For those who are dying, we pray. R.

For scientists, researchers, and all who are working to
conquer disease, we pray. R.

For all who build up the kingdom of God on earth,
we pray. R.

PRAYER

The leader concludes the intercessions with a prayer.

Leader: Father of our Lord Jesus Christ,
    your Son accepted suffering
    to teach us the virtue of patience in human illness.
    Hear the prayers we offer for our sick brother/sister.
    May all who suffer pain, illness, or disease
    realize that they have been chosen to be saints
    and know that they are joined to Christ
    in his suffering for the salvation of the world.

    We ask this through Christ our Lord.

All: Amen.

Or:

Leader: All-powerful and ever-living God,
    the lasting health of all who believe in you,
    hear us as we ask your loving help for the sick;
    restore their health,
    that they may again offer joyful thanks
    in your Church.

    Grant this through Christ our Lord.

All: Amen.

Or:

Leader: Loving God,
    you love us more fully than we can imagine.
    Help us to remember
    how you show us your love in Jesus,
    and teach us to love you
    by loving and serving one another.

    We ask this grace through Jesus Christ our Lord.

All: Amen.

Leader: We bless you, God of all consolation,
and give you glory and praise.
In the midst of the challenges of life
you reveal your power and strength,
shining through our human weakness.

We turn to you in all our troubles
and praise you in our times of joy.
Above all we thank you
for the death and resurrection of Jesus
who gives us faith and hope
as we journey to your kingdom.

Give us your strength to love and serve others
as Jesus did in his days on earth.
Fill us with your Spirit of compassion,
to reach out to those in need.

Glory, honor, and praise to you, loving God,
in the Church and in Christ Jesus,
with the Holy Spirit, for ever and ever.

All: Amen.

Or:

For Family or Friends

Leader: Lord Jesus,
we rejoice in your loving kindness
that is revealed to *N.*
in the support and love of
his/her (family/friends/neighbors).
Renew and strengthen their love
by the presence of Jesus
who gave his life upon the cross
for the salvation of the world.
Support them in this difficult time
with your joy and peace each day.

Lord Jesus, hear our prayer,
for you are Lord, for ever and ever.

All: Amen.

THE LORD'S PRAYER

The leader introduces the Lord's Prayer in these or similar words.

Leader: Now let us offer together the prayer
our Lord Jesus Christ taught us:

All: Our Father....

BLESSING

The leader prays a blessing.

Leader: All praise and glory is yours, Lord our God,
for you have called us to serve you in love.
Bless *N.*,
so that he/she may bear this illness
in union with your Son's obedient suffering.
Restore him/her to health,
and lead him/her to glory.

We ask this through Christ our Lord.

All: Amen.

For an Elderly Person

Leader: All praise and glory are yours, Lord our God,
for you have called us to serve you in love.
Bless all who have grown old in your service
and give *N.* strength and courage
to continue to follow Jesus your Son.

We ask this through Christ our Lord.

All: Amen.

If possible (healthy condition), it may be appropriate that the senior member of a family bless those visiting him/her, if it is requested by them. Then all may exchange a sign of peace.

Or, making the sign of the cross on him/herself, the leader may say:

Leader: May the Lord bless us,
protect us from all evil,
and bring us to everlasting life.

All: Amen.

CONCLUSION

All may exchange a sign of peace.

Other Prayers with the Sick

For a Sick Person

Leader: Lord Jesus, our Savior and our brother,
listen to our prayer and look with love on N..
Visit him/her in this time of sickness
and fill him/her with the gifts of your Spirit,
that he/she may have the courage to carry your cross,
the strength to believe in your love,
and the faith to persevere in hope and prayer.
(Restore his/her strength
and bring him/her back to full health.)

Lord Jesus, unite our prayer to your own,
and present it to God most high.
To God be glory and praise for ever and ever.

All: Amen.

For a Sick Child

Leader: Heavenly Father, you love us all.
Have mercy on us and listen to our prayer
as we ask you to help N..
Bless him/her, for he/she is your beloved child.

We ask this grace in the name of Jesus the Lord.

All: Amen.

Before Surgery

Leader: Lord Jesus, be with N.
as he/she prepares for this operation.
In your love, guard and protect him/her.
Through the skills of the doctors,
the care of the nurses and staff,
and the constant prayers
of all his/her family and friends,
bring him/her back to health
and quickly restore him/her to full activity.

Lord Jesus, we thank you
for your healing love and saving action
among your people.
Through you be glory and praise to God our Father
in the power of the Holy Spirit for ever and ever.

All: Amen.

After Surgery

Leader: Loving God,
we give you praise and glory
for we know that you constantly watch over us
and keep us close to you.
We thank you for granting N. a safe recovery,
and commend him/her again to your enduring care.
Embrace N. in your mercy and love,
and continue the healing process
until he/she is restored to full health.

Glory and honor and praise are yours,
through Jesus Christ our Lord,
in the love of your Holy Spirit,
one God, for ever and ever.

All: Amen.

For All the Sick

Leader: Jesus our Lord,
we ask you to have mercy on all who are sick.
Give them your strength and love,
and help them to carry this cross with faith.
May their sufferings be one with yours,
overcome the power of evil,
and lead others to our Father in heaven.
Lord Jesus, hear our prayer,
for you are Lord for ever and ever.

All: Amen.

For the Chronically Ill

Leader: Loving God,
rock of strength for those who trust in you;
comforter of those who call on you.
Hear the cry of those who suffer
from constant sickness or weakness,
and embrace them in your loving arms.
As you have united them to the suffering of Christ
in the waters of baptism,
be their companion on the way of the cross,
give them peace,
and strengthen them with the vision of your kingdom.

We make this prayer through Jesus Christ our Lord.

All: Amen.

For the Terminally Ill

Leader: Lord Jesus, our brother,
have pity on those who suffer for love of you.
As they carry their cross each day with you,
let them share in your mission to save the world
by their patient and prayerful endurance.

Give them strength in their time of weakness,
and peace in the midst of anxiety,
until they embrace the fullness of the paschal mystery
in the glory of your kingdom,
where you live and reign for ever and ever.

All: Amen.

For Those Who Care for the Sick

Leader: Lord Jesus, our brother,
you showed your compassion for the sick
when you reached out in love to them.
We praise you for the saving love
that is exercised among those who care for the sick.
Conform them more and more to your image
that they may be your healing touch to the sick,
and share the peace
of your Holy Spirit with all they meet.

Glory and praise to you, Christ Jesus,
the incarnation of the Father's love,
you are Lord for ever and ever.

All: Amen.

VISITING A SICK CHILD

In the room of the child who is sick, it is helpful to have a Bible, New Testament, or book of psalms; a container of blessed water; and a cross, holy picture, or statue.

When a child is seriously sick, parents, brothers and sisters, relatives, friends, and neighbors may want to pray together for him or her. A child who is old enough to understand may wish to join them in prayer.

This prayer service may be celebrated in the hospital room; it may be used in the hospital chapel, at home, or in the parish church.

Any of the prayers may be adapted according to circumstances.

INTRODUCTION

The visitors greet the child and his/her parents and family, and, if unknown, introduce themselves. The visitors may then speak quietly with the sick child and his/her parents.

One of them may begin a time of prayer with the sign of the cross and a greeting. The leader may say:

Leader: *N.*, trust in the Lord, for God is always with you.

SCRIPTURE READING

One of the following readings may be chosen.

Leader: Let us listen to these words from Scripture.

Reader: Jesus and his disciples came to Capernaum;
and when Jesus was in the house he asked them,
"What were you arguing about on the way?"

But they were silent, for on the way they had argued
with one another who was the greatest.
He sat down, called the twelve, and said to them,
"Whoever wants to be first
must be last of all and servant of all."

Then he took a little child and put it among them;
and taking it in his arms, he said to them,
"Whoever welcomes one such child in my name
welcomes me,
and whoever welcomes me
welcomes not me but the one who sent me."

Mark 9.33-37

Or:

Reader: People were bringing little children to Jesus
in order that he might touch them;
and his disciples spoke sternly to them.

But when Jesus saw this,
he was indignant and said to them,
"Let the little children come to me; do not stop them;
for it is to such as these
that the kingdom of God belongs.
Truly I tell you,
whoever does not receive the kingdom of God
as a little child will never enter it."
And he took them up in his arms,
laid his hands on them, and blessed them.

Mark 10.13-16

Or: *Mark* 6.54-56 (page 149).

This may be followed by a moment of silent prayer.

LITANY

The leader may help the child and family to respond to the Scripture reading with the following petitions. All may repeat them after the leader.

Leader: Jesus, come to me.

All: Jesus, come to me.

Leader: Jesus, put your hand on me.

All: Jesus, put your hand on me.

Leader: Jesus, bless me.

All: Jesus, bless me.

Leader: Jesus, strengthen me (heal me).

All: Jesus, strengthen me (heal me).

Leader: Jesus, comfort my family (parents).

All: Jesus, comfort my family (parents).

PRAYER

The leader concludes the intercessions with a prayer.

Leader: God of love,
ever caring, ever strong,
stand by us in our time of need.
Watch over your child N., who is sick,
look after him/her in every danger,
and grant him/her your healing and peace.

We ask this in the name of Jesus the Lord.

All: Amen.

Or:

Leader: Father,
in your love you gave us Jesus
to help us rise triumphant over grief and pain.
Look on your child *N.* who is sick
and see in his/her sufferings those of your Son.
Grant *N.* a share in the strength you granted your Son
that he/she too may be a sign
of your goodness, kindness, and loving care.

We ask this in the name of Jesus the Lord.

All: Amen.

THE LORD'S PRAYER

The leader introduces the Lord's Prayer in these or similar words.

Leader: Now let us offer together the prayer
our Lord Jesus Christ taught us:

All: Our Father....

BLESSING

The leader makes the sign of the cross on the child's forehead.

Leader: *N.*, when you were baptized,
you were marked with the cross of Jesus.
I (We) make this cross ✠ on your forehead
and ask the Lord to bless you,
and restore you to health.

All: Amen.

Or:

Leader: All praise and glory is yours, Lord,
for you have called us to serve you in love.
Have mercy on us and listen to our prayer
as we ask you to help N..
Bless ✠ your beloved child,
and restore him/her to health
in the name of Jesus the Lord.

All: Amen.

If desired, the parents and others present may trace the sign of the cross on the child's forehead, in silence.

CONCLUSION

Making the sign of the cross on him/herself, the leader may say:

Leader: May the Lord bless us,
protect us from all evil,
and bring us to everlasting life.

All: Amen.

Communion of the Sick

Those who are sick are deprived of their accustomed place in the eucharistic community. In bringing Communion, ministers of Communion represent Christ and show the faith and love of the community. Communion to the sick is a sign of support and concern by God's people for those who are ill.

The sick should have the opportunity of receiving Holy Communion frequently, even daily. Extra-ordinary ministers will be the normal means for achieving this.

When Holy Communion is brought, it is useful to have a table covered with a cloth and with a lighted candle near the bed of the sick person. A glass of water is also helpful. Family and friends are invited and encouraged to take an active part in the celebration.

If the sick person wishes to go to confession, it is preferable that this take place at an earlier visit by a priest. Reconciliation may also take place at the penitential rite, which is then omitted.

When the sick person is unable to receive under the form of bread, it may be given to him/her under the form of wine alone.

> May the Lord Jesus Christ protect you
> and lead you to eternal life.

About the Eucharistic Fast

The sick (at home or in hospital, even if not bedridden), the elderly and the dying are exempt from the eucharistic fast. They may receive communion even if they have had something to eat or drink within the previous hour.

Outline of the Rite of Communion of the Sick

Introductory rites
Greeting
Sprinkling with holy water
Penitential rite

Liturgy of the Word
Reading
Response
General Intercessions

Liturgy of Holy Communion
Lord's Prayer
Communion
Silent prayer
Prayer after Communion

Concluding rite
Blessing

When Communion is brought as Viaticum, the "Baptismal Profession of Faith" and Litany conclude the Liturgy of the Word.

For the celebration of the Communion of the Sick, see *Communion of the Sick, Ritual and Pastoral Notes for Lay Ministers* (1996) pages 9-30.

Blessing God
at the Time
of Death

For Christians, death is not the end, but the beginning of new and eternal life. In death, we are brought into the fullness of the paschal mystery of Christ; we complete our union with Jesus, a union that began when we were baptized. It is the tradition of the Catholic Church to pray for those whom God has called into eternity. We are united with them in Christ and through our baptism and our faith.

The Church's basic prayers for the dead and for those who mourn them in faith, hope, and love are contained in the ritual book, *Order of Christian Funerals*.

For the celebration of Viaticum, see *Communion of the Sick, Ritual and Pastoral Notes for Lay Ministers* (1996) pages 31-45.

FOR THE DYING

When God calls us in death, we enter fully into the paschal mystery of Jesus' dying and rising; our baptism is fulfilled.

Prayers for the dying are contained the ritual book *Pastoral Care of the Sick*.

SHORT TEXTS

One or more of the following texts drawn from Scripture may be recited with the dying person. They may be softly repeated two or three times.

Who can separate us from the love of Christ? *Romans* 8.35

Whether we live or die, we are the Lord's. *Romans* 14.8

We have an everlasting home in heaven. *2 Corinthians* 5.1

We shall be with the Lord for ever. *1 Thessalonians* 4.17

We shall see God as he really is. *1 John* 3.2

We have passed from death to life because we love each other. *1 John* 3.14

To you, Lord, I lift up my soul. *Psalm* 25.1

The Lord is my light and my salvation. *Psalm* 27.1

I believe that I shall see the goodness of the Lord
in the land of the living. *Psalm* 27.13

My soul thirsts for the living God. *Psalm* 42.3

Though I walk in the shadow of death, I will fear no evil,
for you are with me. *Psalm* 23.4

Come, blessed of my Father, says the Lord Jesus,
and take possession of the kingdom prepared for you. *Matthew* 25.34

The Lord Jesus says, today you will be with me in paradise. *Luke* 23.43

In my Father's home there are many dwelling places,
says the Lord Jesus. *John* 14.2

The Lord Jesus says, I go to prepare a place for you,
and I will come again to take you to myself. *John* 14.2-3

I desire that where I am, they also may be with me,
says the Lord Jesus. *John* 17.24

Everyone who believes in the Son has eternal life. *John* 6.40

Into your hands, Lord, I commend my spirit. *Psalm* 31.5a

Lord Jesus, receive my spirit. *Acts* 7.59

Holy Mary, pray for me.
Saint Joseph, pray for me,
Jesus, Mary and Joseph, assist me in my last agony.

LONGER TEXTS FROM SCRIPTURE

Job	19.23-27 *he will rise up last, on the dust of the earth;*
Psalm	23 *the Good Shepherd;* or 25 *prayer for God's favor and protection;* or 91 *safe in God's sheltering care;*
1 John	4.4-16 *we are from God;*
Revelation	21.1-5a, 6-7 *a new heaven and a new earth;*
Matthew	25.1-13 *parable of the ten wedding attendants;*
Luke	22.39-46 *pray not to be put to the test;* or 23.44-49 *Father, into your hands I commit my spirit;* or 24.1-8 *the empty tomb;*
John	6.37-40 *whoever believes in the Son will have eternal life;* or 14.1-6, 23, 27 *I am going to prepare a place for you.*

LITANY OF THE SAINTS

When the condition of the dying person invites the use of brief forms of prayer, those who are present are encouraged to pray the litany of the saints – or at least some of its invocations – for him or her.

Special mention may be made of the patron saints of the dying person, of the family, and of the parish.

Leader: All:

Lord, have mercy,   Lord, have mercy.
Christ, have mercy,   Christ, have mercy.
Lord, have mercy,   Lord, have mercy.

Holy Mary, Mother of God,   pray for him/her.
Saint Michael,
Holy angels of God,

Abraham, Moses and Elijah   pray for him/her.
Saint Joachim and Saint Anne
Saint Joseph,
Saint John the Baptist,
Saint Peter and Saint Paul,
Saint Andrew,
Saint John,
Saint Mary Magdalene,

Saint Stephen,   pray for him/her.
Saint Ignatius,
Saint Lawrence,
Saint Perpetua and Saint Felicity,
Saint Agnes,
Saint Isaac Jogues and Saint René Goupil,

Saint Gregory,   pray for him/her.
Saint Augustine,
Saint Athanasius,
Saint Basil,
Saint Catherine of Siena,
Saint Teresa of Avila,
Saint Martin,
Saint John Neumann,

Saint Benedict,	pray for him/her.
Saint Francis and Saint Dominic,	
Saint Francis Xavier,	
Saint John Vianney,	
Saints Elizabeth Ann Seton,	
Rose Philippine Duchesne, Mother Théodore Guérin,	
Frances Xavier Cabrini, Katharine Drexel,	

Saint Monica,	pray for him/her.
Saint Louis,	
Blessed Kateri Tekakwitha,	

Patron saints of the dying person, of the family and of the parish; and saints to whom the dying person may have a special devotion may also be included.

All holy men and women,	pray for him/her.

Lord, be merciful,	Lord, save your people.
From all harm,	
From every sin,	
From all temptations,	
From everlasting death,	
By your coming among us,	
By your death and rising to new life,	
By your gift of the Holy Spirit,	

Be merciful to us sinners,	Lord, hear our prayer.

Bring *N.* to eternal life,
   first promised to him/her in baptism,

Raise *N.* on the last day,
   for he/she has eaten the bread of life,

Let *N.* share in your glory,
   for he/she has shared
   in your suffering and death,

Jesus, Son of the living God,

Christ, hear us,	Christ, hear us.
Lord Jesus, hear our prayer,	Lord Jesus, hear our prayer.

Or:

A brief form of the litany may be prayed.

Leader: All:

Holy Mary, Mother of God,   pray for him/her.
Holy angels of God,
Saint Joseph,
Saint John the Baptist,
Saint Peter and Saint Paul,

Other saints may be added, especially particular patrons.

All holy men and women,   pray for him/her.

Or, other customary prayers may be used.

Then, the leader may conclude:

Leader: God of power and mercy,
         you have made death itself
         the gateway to eternal life.
         Look with love on our dying brother (sister),
         and make him (her) one with your Son
         in his suffering and death,
         that, sealed with the blood of Christ,
         he (she) may come before you free from sin.

         We ask this through Christ our Lord.

         (Sacramentary n. 543)

PRAYERS OF COMMENDATION

When the moment of death seems near, some of the following prayers may be said:

Leader: Go forth, Christian soul, from this world
in the name of God the almighty Father,
who created you,
in the name of Jesus Christ, Son of the living God,
who suffered for you,
in the name of the Holy Spirit,
who was poured out upon you.
Go forth, faithful Christian.

May you live in peace this day,
may your home be with God in Zion,
with Mary, the virgin Mother of God,
with Joseph, and all the angels and saints.

Or:

Leader: I commend you, my dear brother/sister,
to almighty God,
and entrust you to your Creator.
May you return to him
who formed you from the dust of the earth.
May holy Mary, the angels,
and all the saints come to meet you
as you go forth from this life.
May Christ who was crucified for you
bring you freedom and peace.
May Christ who died for you
admit you into his garden of paradise.
May Christ, the true Shepherd,
acknowledge you as one of his flock. ➤

May he forgive all your sins,
and set you among those he has chosen.
May you see your Redeemer face to face,
and enjoy the vision of God for ever.

All: Amen.

Or:

Leader: Welcome your servant, Lord,
into the place of salvation
which because of your mercy
he/she rightly hoped for.

All: R. Amen.

Or:

R. Lord, save your people.

Leader: Deliver your servant, Lord, from every distress. R.

Deliver your servant, Lord,
as you delivered Noah from the flood. R.

Deliver your servant, Lord,
as you delivered Abraham from Ur of the Chaldeans. R.

Deliver your servant, Lord,
as you delivered Job from his sufferings. R.

Deliver your servant, Lord,
as you delivered Moses
from the hand of the Pharaoh. R.

Deliver your servant, Lord,
as you delivered Daniel from the den of lions. R.

Deliver your servant, Lord,
as you delivered the three young men
from the fiery furnace. R.

Deliver your servant, Lord,
as you delivered Susanna from her false accusers. R.

Deliver your servant, Lord,
as you delivered David
from the attacks of Saul and Goliath. R.

Deliver your servant, Lord,
as you delivered Peter and Paul from prison. R.

Deliver your servant, Lord,
through Jesus our Savior,
who suffered death for us and gave us eternal life. R.

CONCLUSION

The following prayer may conclude the litany:

Leader: Lord Jesus Christ, Savior of the world,
we pray for your servant N.,
and commend him/her to your mercy.
For his/her sake you came down from heaven;
receive him/her now into the joy of your kingdom.
For though he/she has sinned,
he/she has not denied the Father,
the Son, and the Holy Spirit,
but has believed in God
and has worshipped his/her Creator.

All: Amen.

The following Marian antiphon may be said or sung.

All: Hail, holy Queen, Mother of mercy,
hail, our life, our sweetness, and our hope.
To you we cry, the children of Eve;
to you we send up our sighs,
mourning and weeping in this land of exile.
Turn, then, most gracious advocate,
your eyes of mercy toward us;
lead us home at last
and show us the blessed fruit of your womb, Jesus:
O clement, O loving, O sweet Virgin Mary.

PRAYERS AT THE TIME OF DEATH

The following prayers may be used as suitable and may be adapted as needed. Prayers from the Commendation of the Dying, may be repeated immediately after death. One of the following responsories may also be said. The mourners may repeat the phrases after the leader.

Leader: In you, Lord, is our hope.
We shall never hope in vain.

All: In you, Lord, is our hope.
We shall never hope in vain.

Leader: We shall be glad and rejoice in your mercy.

All: We shall be glad and rejoice in your mercy.

Leader: We shall never hope in vain.

All: We shall never hope in vain.

Leader: Glory to the Father, and to the Son,
and to the Holy Spirit.

All: Glory to the Father, and to the Son,
and to the Holy Spirit.

Leader: In you, Lord, is our hope.
We shall never hope in vain.

All: In you, Lord, is our hope.
We shall never hope in vain.

Or:

The Events that Surround Death

Leader: Lord, in your steadfast love,
give him/her/them eternal rest.

All: Lord, in your steadfast love,
give him/her/them eternal rest.

Leader: You will come to judge the living and the dead.

All: You will come to judge the living and the dead.

Leader: Give him/her/them eternal rest.

All: Give him/her/them eternal rest.

Leader: Glory to the Father, and to the Son,
and to the Holy Spirit.

All: Glory to the Father, and to the Son,
and to the Holy Spirit.

Leader: Lord, in your steadfast love,
give him/her/them eternal rest.

All: Lord, in your steadfast love,
give him/her/them eternal rest.

Or:

Leader: May the angels lead you into paradise;
may the martyrs come to welcome you
and take you to the holy city,
the new and eternal Jerusalem.

May choirs of angels welcome you
and lead you to the bosom of Abraham:
and where Lazarus is poor no longer
may you find eternal rest.

Or:

Leader: Lord Jesus, our Redeemer,
you willingly gave yourself up to death
so that all people might be saved
and pass from death to new life.
Listen to our prayers,
look with love on your people
who mourn and pray for their brother/sister *N.*.

Lord Jesus, holy and compassionate:
forgive *N.* his/her sins.
By dying you opened the gates of life
for those who believe in you:
do not let our brother/sister be parted from you,
but by your glorious power
give him/her light, joy and peace in heaven
where you live forever and ever.

All: Amen.

PRAYERS AFTER DEATH

This prayer service may be celebrated after the death of a family member. The parish priest, chaplain or pastoral care worker, a member of the family or a friend may lead the prayer.

SIGN OF THE CROSS

All make the sign of the cross as the leader says:

Leader: In the name of the Father, and of the Son, ✠ and of the Holy Spirit.

All: Amen.

INVITATION TO PRAYER

Using one of the following invitations, or in similar words, the leader invites those present to pray.

Leader: In this moment of sorrow
the Lord is in our midst
and consoles us with his word.
As we prepare to hear God's word,
let us pray in silence.

Or:

Leader: Let us ask the God of all consolation
to open our hearts to his word,
so that listening to it, we may comfort one another,
find light in time of darkness,
and faith in time of doubt.

All reflect in silence.

SCRIPTURE READING

The leader or one of those present proclaims the reading.
One or more of the following may be used.

Leader: Let us listen to these words from Scripture.

Reader: Jesus said:
"Truly I tell you,
if two of you agree on earth about anything you ask,
it will be done for you by my Father in heaven.
For where two or three are gathered in my name,
I am there among them."

Matthew 18.19-20

Or:

Reader: Martha said to Jesus,
"Lord, if you had been here,
my brother would not have died.
But even now I know that God
will give you whatever you ask of him."

Jesus said to her,
"Your brother will rise again."

Martha said to him,
"I know that he will rise again
in the resurrection on the last day."

Jesus said to her,
"I am the resurrection and the life.
Those who believe in me, even though they die, will live,
and everyone who lives and believes in me
will never die. Do you believe this?"

She said to him,
"Yes, Lord, I believe that you are the Messiah,
the Son of God, the one coming into the world."

John 11. 21-17

Or:

Reader: Jesus said:
"Come to me,
all you that are weary and are carrying heavy burdens,
and I will give you rest.
Take my yoke upon you, and learn from me;
for I am gentle and humble in heart,
and you will find rest for your souls.
For my yoke is easy, and my burden is light."

Matthew 11.28-30

Or:

Reader: Jesus said:
"This is indeed the will of my Father,
that all who see the Son and believe in him
may have eternal life;
and I will raise them up on the last day."

John 6.40

Or:

Reader: Jesus said, "Do not let your hearts be troubled.
Believe in God, believe also in me.
In my Father's house there are many dwelling places.
If it were not so, would I have told you
that I go to prepare a place for you?
And if I go and prepare a place for you,
I will come again and will take you to myself,
so that where I am, there you may be also.

John 14.1-3

Or:

Reader: I, John, heard a voice from heaven say to me,
"Write this:
Blessed are the dead who from now on die in the Lord."
"Yes," says the Spirit, "they will rest from their labors,
for their deeds follow them."

cf. *Revelation* 14.13

Pause for silent prayer.

THE LORD'S PRAYER

The leader invites those present to pray the Lord's Prayer.

Leader: With God there is mercy and fullness of redemption;
let us pray as Jesus taught us:

All: Our Father....

CONCLUDING PRAYERS

A prayer for the deceased person is then said.
This prayer may be followed by a prayer for the mourners.

For the Deceased Person

Leader: Almighty God,
by the mystery of the cross,
you have made us strong;
by the sacrament of the resurrection
you have sealed us as your own.
Look kindly upon your servant *N.*,
now freed from the bonds of mortality,
and count him/her among your saints in heaven.

We ask this through Christ our Lord.

All: Amen.

Or:

Leader: Into your hands, O Lord,
we humbly entrust our brother/sister *N.*.
In this life you embraced him/her
with your tender love;
deliver him/her now from every evil
and bid him/her enter eternal rest.

The old order has passed away:
welcome him/her into paradise,
where there will be no sorrow,
no weeping nor pain,
but the fullness of peace and joy
with your Son and the Holy Spirit for ever and ever.

All: Amen.

For the Mourners

Leader: Lord God,
you are attentive to the voice of our pleading.
Let us find in your Son
comfort in our sadness,
certainty in our doubt,
and courage to live through this hour.
Make our faith strong through Christ our Lord.

All: Amen.

Or:

Leader: Most merciful God,
whose wisdom is beyond our understanding,
surround the family of N. with your love,
that they may not be overwhelmed by their loss,
but have confidence in your goodness,
and strength to meet the days to come.

We ask this through Christ our Lord.

All: Amen.

Responsorial Prayer

Leader: Blessed are those who have died in the Lord;
let them rest from their labors
for their good deeds go with them.
Eternal rest grant unto him/her, O Lord.

All: And let perpetual light shine upon him/her.

Leader: May he/she rest in peace.

All: Amen.

Leader: May his/her soul
and the souls of all the faithful departed,
through the mercy of God, rest in peace.

All: Amen.

Blessing

A priest or deacon blesses those present as usual.
A lay leader invokes God's blessing and makes the sign of the cross, on himself or herself, saying:

Leader: May the love of God
and the peace of the Lord Jesus Christ
bless and console us
and gently wipe every tear from our eyes:
In the name of the Father, and of the Son, ✠
and of the Holy Spirit.

All: Amen.

PRAYERS WITH PARENTS
AFTER A CHILD HAS DIED
OR AFTER A MISCARRIAGE

When a baby is stillborn, or dies before the celebration of baptism, the parents may seek the prayers of the Church. In the meantime, the following readings and prayers may be used with the prayers given above.

INTRODUCTION

All make the sign of the cross as the leader begins:

Leader: In the name of the Father, and of the Son, ✠
and of the Holy Spirit.

All: Amen.

SCRIPTURE READING

One or more of the following passages may be read.

Leader: Let us listen to these words from Scripture.

Reader: All who are led by the Spirit of God are children of God.
For you did not receive
a spirit of slavery to fall back into fear,
but you have received a spirit of adoption.

When we cry, "Abba! Father!"
it is that very Spirit bearing witness with our spirit
that we are children of God,
and if children, then heirs,
heirs of God and joint heirs with Christ –
if, in fact, we suffer with him
so that we may also be glorified with him.

Romans 8.14-17

Or:

Death of a Child / Miscarriage

Reader: My brothers and sisters,
whenever you face trials of any kind,
consider it nothing but joy, because you know
that the testing of your faith produces endurance;
and let endurance have its full effect,
so that you may be mature and complete,
lacking in nothing.

James 1.2-4

Or:

Reader: Jesus said: "Come to me,
all you who labor and are overburdened,
and I will give you rest.
Shoulder my yoke and learn from me,
for I am gentle and humble in heart,
and you will find rest for your souls.
Yes, my yoke is easy and my burden light."

cf. *Matthew 11.28-30*

Or:

Reader: Jesus said to his disciples:
"Do not let your hearts be troubled.
Trust in God still, and trust in me.
There are many rooms in my Father's house;
if there were not, I should have told you.
I am going now to prepare a place for you,
and after I have gone and prepared you a place
I shall return to take you with me;
so that where I am you may be too."

cf. *John 14.1-3*

Or:

Other Passages:

Romans   5.1-8 *faith guarantees salvation; or* 8.1-6 *we direct our lives by the Spirit;
or* 8.9-11 *the spirit is alive because you have been justified; or* 8.26-32 *the
Spirit comes to help us in our weakness; or* 8.28-39 *can anything cut us off
from the love of Christ?;*

Ephesians	1.3-14 *God's plan of salvation;* or 3.15-23 *the triumph and the supremacy of Christ;*
Hebrews	5.7-10 *he offered up prayer to the one who had the power to save him from death;*
James	1.12-18 *receiving the Word and putting it into practice;*
Matthew	5.1-10 *the Beatitudes;* or 6.7-15 *how to pray–the Lord's Prayer;* or 11.25-30 *come to me and you will find rest for your soul;* or 25.31-40 *the last judgment;*
Mark	4.35-41 *the calming of the storm;* or 10.46-52 *the blind man of Jericho;*
Luke	2.22-35 *Jesus is presented in the Temple;* or 4.16-22b *Jesus at Nazareth;* or 6.17-23 *the crowds follow Jesus;* or 8.19-21 *the true family of Jesus;* or 9.22-26 *whoever loses their life for the sake of Jesus will find it;* or 22.39-46 *Father, let your will be done, not mine;* or 24.13-32 *the road to Emmaus;*
John	10.11-18 *the Good Shepherd lays down his life for his sheep;* or 15.1-11 *the true vine;* or 17.1-13 *the prayer of Jesus.*

INTERCESSIONS

The following intentions may be prayed by one of those present or by the leader. All may respond with a familiar refrain, such as "Lord, hear our prayer" or with a moment of silence.

Reader: May the Father of mercies comfort you with peace,
(we pray. *R.*)

May the God of hope, who raised Jesus from the dead,
strengthen and raise your spirits, (we pray. *R.*)

May Christ Jesus, who was born as a little child,
embrace you in his love, (we pray. *R.*)

May Jesus, who welcomed little children,
receive your child into his arms, (we pray. *R.*)

May Jesus, who appeared to his disciples on the road
to Emmaus, reveal his presence to you, (we pray. *R.*)

May the Virgin Mary, who stood at the foot of her Son's
cross, help you with strength and consolation,
(we pray. *R.*)

May the Mother of Jesus and our Mother, now care for
your child in heaven, (we pray. *R.*)   ➤

May the angels guide your child to our Father's home, (we pray. *R.*)

May the saints surround your child as many brothers and sisters in Christ, (we pray. *R.*)

Prayer

The leader concludes the intentions with an appropriate prayer.

For a Miscarriage

Leader: God of mercy and consolation,
you are the Lord of the living and the dead:
in you alone is found all life and meaning.
Hear our cry this day
as we turn to you in our time of sorrow and loss.
We pray for these parents
who have lost the love of their life:
their dreams and hopes for the future.
Fill their wounded hearts with consolation
and heal their spirits.
Receive the soul of their child
into your kingdom of happiness and peace
to grow and mature in your presence.
For us who remain on earth,
receive our tears as a sign of our love
and give us the strength and courage
to believe that you will bring goodness
out of every situation.

We make our prayer through Jesus Christ,
your Son and our Lord,
who lives with you and the Holy Spirit
in the light of heaven for ever and ever.

All: Amen.

For a Stillborn Child

Leader: Lord God,
ever caring and gentle,
we commit to your love this little one,
quickened to life for so short a time.
Enfold him/her in eternal life.
We pray for his/her parents
who are saddened by the loss of their baby.
Give them courage
and help them in their pain and grief.
May they all meet one day
in the joy and peace of your kingdom.

We ask this through Christ our Lord.

All:　　 Amen.

For a Child

Leader: To you, O Lord,
we humbly entrust this child,
so precious in your sight.
Take him/her into your arms
and welcome him/her into paradise,
where there will be no sorrow, no weeping, no pain,
but the fullness of peace and joy
with your Son and the Holy Spirit
for ever and ever.

All:　　 Amen.

Or:

Leader: God of all consolation,
searcher of mind and heart,
the faith of these parents (*N.* and *N.*) is known to you.
Comfort them with the knowledge
that the child for whom they grieve
is entrusted now to your loving care.

We ask this through Christ our Lord.

All: Amen.

CONCLUSION

All may recite the Lord's Prayer and exchange a sign of peace.

ORDER OF CHRISTIAN FUNERALS

The following prayers and outlines of the liturgies for the burial of the dead will assist families in the preparation and celebration of the funeral liturgies.

GATHERING IN THE PRESENCE OF THE BODY

This rite may be used when the family arrives at the funeral home and views the body of their loved one.

SIGN OF THE CROSS

All present sign themselves with the sign of the cross as the leader says:

Leader: In the name of the Father, and of the Son, ✠ and of the Holy Spirit.

All: Amen.

SCRIPTURE READING

One of those present proclaims the reading.

Leader: Let us listen to these words of Scripture.

Reader: Jesus said to the disciples:
"I will not leave you orphaned;
I am coming to you.
In a little while the world will no longer see me,
but you will see me;
because I live, you also will live."

cf. *John* 14.18-19

Or:

Reader: We do not live to ourselves,
and we do not die to ourselves.
If we live, we live to the Lord,
and if we die, we die to the Lord;
so then, whether we live or whether we die,
we are the Lord's.
For to this end Christ died and lived again,
so that he might be Lord of both the dead and the living.

Romans 14.7-9

Or:

Reader: Here is a saying that you can rely on:
If we have died with him, we will also live with him;
If we endure, we will also reign with him;
If we deny him, he will also deny us;
If we are faithless, he remains faithful –
for he cannot deny himself.

cf. *2 Timothy* 2.11-13

Or:

Reader: I, John, heard a voice from heaven say to me,
"Write this:
Blessed are the dead who from now on die in the Lord."
"Yes," says the Spirit, "they will rest from their labors,
for their deeds follow them."

cf. *Revelation* 14.13

THE LORD'S PRAYER

The leader introduces the Lord's Prayer in these or similar words.

Leader: With God there is mercy and fullness of redemption;
let us pray as Jesus taught us:

All: Our Father....

Concluding Prayer

The leader says one of the following prayers.

Leader: Almighty God and Father,
it is our certain faith
that your Son, who died on the cross,
was raised from the dead,
the firstfruits of all who have fallen asleep.
Grant that through this mystery
your servant N.,
who has gone to his/her rest in Christ,
may share in the joy of his resurrection.

We ask this through Christ our Lord.

All: Amen.

Or:

Leader: Blessed are those who have died in the Lord;
let them rest from their labors
for their good deeds go with them.
Eternal rest grant unto him/her O Lord.

All: And let perpetual light shine upon him/her.

Leader: May he/she rest in peace.

All: Amen.

Leader: May his/her soul
and the souls of all the faithful departed,
through the mercy of God rest in peace.

All: Amen.

Or:

Leader: May the love of God and peace of the Lord Jesus Christ
bless and console us
and gently wipe every tear from our eyes.

All: Amen.

PLANNING THE FUNERAL MASS

"Christians celebrate the funeral rites to offer worship, praise, and thanksgiving to God for the gift of life which has now been returned to God, the author of life and hope of the just. The Mass, the memorial of Christ's death and resurrection, is the principal celebration of the Christian funeral." *(OCF,* no. 5)

When planning the Funeral Mass,
there are a number of points to consider:

A Funeral Mass is celebrated for every deceased Catholic in the parish church.

The Mass may be celebrated on any day except during the Easter Triduum (the days between Holy Thursday and Easter Sunday) or on a Sunday or a Holy Day of Obligation. In the case of the Triduum, the burial may take place in the context of a word service with a Mass celebrated after the Triduum.

If families do not wish to have a Mass, they should consult with the parish priest before making any arrangements with the funeral director. If there is serious reason not to celebrate Mass, *The Order of Christian Funerals* (no. 350) states that the service without a Mass is "ordinarily" still to be celebrated in the parish church rather than in the funeral home.

The funeral liturgy emphasizes the baptism of the deceased; it is through baptism in Jesus that each person receives the promise of eternal life. A white pall is draped over the coffin, holy water is sprinkled over the body, and the Easter candle is placed near the coffin in the church. These are the symbols of Christ's life, bestowed through the waters of baptism.

Secular music cannot be accommodated during the Mass; the very nature of the Mass requires that all music at the celebration "express the mystery of the Lord's suffering, death and triumph over death" *(OCF,* no. 30).

The readings for Mass are taken from the Bible. The family may choose the readings (even beyond the passages suggested in the Lectionary) but they must always be from Sacred Scripture.

The *Order of Christian Funerals* prohibits a eulogy in the context of Mass.

"A brief homily based on the readings is always given after the gospel reading at the funeral liturgy but there is never to be a eulogy" (OCF, no. 27). While a eulogy is intended to recall and even praise the deceased, a homily is directed to helping all who are gathered to understand the mystery of God's love. It recalls how the mystery of Jesus' victorious death and resurrection were present in the life of the deceased and are to be reflected in our lives as well. In order to assist the priest in the development of the homily, the family may wish to provide before the Mass some details of the deceased's life, preferably in written form.

A eulogy or "words of remembrance" have an appropriate place at the conclusion of the vigil service at the wake, following the prayers at the cemetery, or at the reception – they are not to be part of the eucharistic celebration. The priest (deacon) will try to incorporate in the homily some points touching the life of the deceased, when they are provided by members of the family.

A souvenir leaflet with biographical and other details of the deceased's life and achievements may be distributed at the time of the funeral. It may also include an outline of the liturgy.

An opportunity to reflect upon the life of the deceased may take place after the vigil service, after the prayers at the cemetery, or at reception following the funeral.

The family of the deceased is encouraged to take an active role in the celebration of the funeral liturgy.

Cremation

In 1984, the Roman Congregation for Divine Worship and the Discipline of the Sacraments granted permission for the funeral liturgy, including the funeral Mass, to be celebrated with the cremated remains of the deceased person present.

This is allowed when the choice of cremation is not inspired by motives contrary to Christian teaching and when the Bishop of the diocese gives permission.

At the funeral Mass, the cremated remains, in a dignified and secure container, are placed on a small table provided for this purpose. The liturgy concludes with the final commendation and the subsequent interment of the remains. The Church asks that in keeping with a spirit of reverence the cremated remains be buried in a grave or entombed in a mausoleum or niche provided for this purpose.

When cremation of the body is chosen by the deceased or by the family as the option for burial, it is recommended that cremation take place after the funeral Mass or liturgy.

RECEPTION OF THE BODY IN THE CHURCH

Placing of the Pall

The members of the family or friends may be the ones to place the white pall over the coffin. The pall symbolizes the baptismal garment, when we "put on" Christ.

LITURGY OF THE WORD

Readings

In consultation with the priest (deacon) the family may select the Scripture readings.

Two or three may be chosen. The gospel is always the last reading, and a psalm is sung after the first reading.

Members of the family or friends may be invited to proclaim the readings before the gospel; members of the parish may also exercise this ministry.

A deacon or priest proclaims the gospel.

Prayer of the Faithful

The family may wish to assist in the preparation of the intercessions. Models and samples are provided in the Ritual Book. The intentions always include petitions for the deceased, the family and the mourners, the Church, and the needs of the world. One or several persons may read the intentions.

The priest invites all to pray before the intentions and concludes with a short prayer.

LITURGY OF THE EUCHARIST

Presentation of the Gifts

Members of the family and/or close friends may bring the bread and wine to be used in the Eucharist to the altar.

Eucharistic Prayer

All present unite themselves with the prayer of the Church, which the priest proclaims. All join in the eucharistic acclamations.

Communion

Communion may be given under both kinds. Since sufficient ministers of Communion will be needed to assist in this ministry, arrangements should be discussed beforehand with the parish priest.

CONCLUDING RITE

Announcements

A member of the family may invite those present to a reception.

Removal of the Pall

The family or others may remove it at the entrance to the church.

Prayers at the End of the Day
After a Celebration for the Deceased

It is fitting for the members of the family to spend a short time of prayer at the end of the day following the vigil for the deceased, the period of visitation, and after the funeral liturgy itself. They may wish to reflect on a brief passage of Scripture or offer familiar prayers before they retire to their homes. The following prayers may be used.

O come, bless the Lord,
all you who serve the Lord,
who stand in the house of the Lord,
in the courts of the house of our God.
Lift up your hands to the holy place
and bless the Lord through the night.
May the Lord bless you from Zion,
he who made both heaven and earth.

cf. *Psalm* 134

Or:

Lord, now you let your servant go in peace;
your word has been fulfilled:
my own eyes have seen the salvation
which you have prepared in the sight of every people:
a light to reveal you to the nations
and the glory of your people Israel.

Luke 2.29-32. Version of the *Liturgy of the Hours.*

Or:

Ever-present and faithful God,
support us all the day long
till the shades lengthen,
and the evening comes
and the busy world is hushed,
and the fever of life is over,
and our work is done!
Then in your mercy give us a safe lodging,
a holy rest, and peace at the last!

Based on a prayer of John Henry Newman.

Responsorial Prayer

Leader: Eternal rest grant unto him/her, O Lord.

All: And let perpetual light shine upon him/her.

Leader: May he/she rest in peace.

All: Amen.

Leader: May his/her soul and the souls
of all the faithful departed,
through the mercy of God, rest in peace.

All: Amen.

Marian Antiphon

The following antiphon may be said or sung.

All: Hail, holy Queen, Mother of mercy,
hail, our life, our sweetness, and our hope.
To you we cry, the children of Eve;
to you we send up our sighs,
mourning and weeping in this land of exile.
Turn, then, most gracious advocate,
your eyes of mercy toward us;
lead us home at last
and show us the blessed fruit of your womb, Jesus:
O clement, O loving, O sweet Virgin Mary.

ANNIVERSARY OF DEATH

Families may observe the anniversary of death of a loved one by arranging to attend the Eucharist at the parish church. They may also observe the anniversary informally at home. Some of the readings and intercessions above may be used. The following prayer may be included.

Leader: Loving God,
listen to our prayers as we remember *N.*
on the anniversary of his/her death.
We thank you for the good things
you have done among us by his/her life and example.
Grant that he/she may rejoice with you in heaven,
as we journey to your kingdom.
Keep us faithful in following the way of Jesus
that we may live in your love.

We ask this through Jesus Christ our Lord.

All: Amen.

WHEN VISITING A CEMETERY

The family may use this prayer or the service on the following page when visiting the graves of family and friends.

Leader: Eternal God,
have mercy on all who are buried here.
(In particular, we pray for *N.* and *N.*)
Bring them into your kingdom of light and peace
and let them share joy with you
and with all your saints.

We ask this through Christ our Lord.

All: Amen.

Or:

Leader: Blessed are those who have died in the Lord;
let them rest from their labors
for their good deeds go with them.
Eternal rest grant unto them, O Lord.

All: And let perpetual light shine upon them.

Leader: May they rest in peace.

All: Amen.

Leader: May their soul and the souls
of all the faithful departed,
through the mercy of God, rest in peace.

All: Amen.

CEMETERY OR MEMORIAL DAY

We respect cemeteries because they are the resting places of the bodies of our beloved dead. In life, these bodies were washed in the waters of baptism and anointed as temples of the Holy Spirit. From death Christ will raise them again into eternal life.

In many communities it is the practice for the people to gather in the cemetery once or twice a year to pray for the dead. The above prayers are suitable for the gathering and may be adapted as necessary. The following prayer may also be used:

Leader: Lord God, wellspring of forgiveness
and loving author of our salvation,
in your mercy hear our prayers
and through the intercessions
of the Blessed Virgin Mary
and all the saints,
bestow on the members of our community,
our friends, relatives, and benefactors
who have passed from this world
a share in your everlasting happiness.

We ask this through Christ our Lord.

All: Amen.

COMMUNITY DISASTER

Suffering loss of life or severe property damage through flood, earthquake, windstorm, snowstorm, or widespread fire, a community may turn to God for help, consolation, and strength.

Some of the prayers and readings suggested above may be used or adapted. The following reading and prayer may be used:

Leader: Let us listen to these words from Scripture.

Reader: I, John, saw a new heaven and a new earth;
for the first heaven and the first earth had passed away,
and the sea was no more.
And I saw the holy city, the new Jerusalem,
coming down out of heaven from God,
prepared as a bride adorned for her husband.
And I heard a loud voice from the throne saying,
"See, the home of God is among mortals.
He will dwell with them as their God;
they will be his peoples,
and God himself will be with them;
he will wipe every tear from their eyes.
Death will be no more;
mourning and crying and pain will be no more,
for the first things have passed away."
And the one who was seated on the throne said,
"See, I am making all things new."

Revelation 21.1-5a

Or:

Other Passages:

Daniel	3.25, 34-43 *the song of Azariah in the furnace;*
Mark	4.35-41 *the calming of the storm;*
Romans	8.31b-39 *a hymn to God's love.*

The leader may offer a brief reflection or invite the present to share a reflection. He invites all to prayer, saying: "Let us pray", so that all may pray silently. Then he says:

Leader: God our Father,
you set the earth on its foundation
and all elements of nature obey your command.
Help us in our time of trouble;
calm the
[flood, earthquake, widespread fire, or other disaster]
that threatens us
and turn our fear of your power
into praise of your goodness.

If people have died:

Have mercy on those who have died
and welcome them into your kingdom of peace and joy.
In your compassion look upon us
and give us tears to mourn their loss.

Let us always feel the presence of your love.
We ask this through Jesus Christ our Lord.

All: Amen.

See: *Sacramentary* nos 544-548.

Or:

AFTER A WINDSTORM OR SNOWSTORM

Leader: Lord Jesus Christ,
when your disciples,
in a middle of a great windstorm on the sea,
woke you up begging for your help and saying,
"Teacher, do you not care that we are perishing?",
you rebuked the wind
and commanded to the sea saying,
"Peace! Be still!"

Hear our cry for help.

Look upon us, we who have been shocked
by a wind/snow storm.

If people have died:

Have mercy on those who have died
and welcome them into your kingdom of peace and joy.
In your compassion look upon us
and give us tears to mourn their loss.

Guide us in the days that lie ahead
and give us strength to rebuild our lives.
Protect us and help us to live for you.
You who live and reign for ever and ever.

All: Amen.

See: Mark 4.35-41

Blessing God during Advent and Christmas

SEASON OF ADVENT

Advent marks the beginning of the liturgical year. It celebrates the three-fold coming of the Lord: remembering the events that surrounded the Lord's coming long ago, celebrating his coming among us today, and looking forward to his final coming in glory. The Advent season recalls the hope of the Christian people as they await the fulfillment or realization of the kingdom of God, inaugurated by Jesus. We await his second coming in glory to gather together the peoples of all nations. Thus it is a season of devout and joyful expectation.

Advent is divided into two periods:

- The first part from the First Sunday of Advent to December 16, focuses on Christ's second coming at the end of time.

- The second part from December 17 to 24, begins the preparation for celebrating the birth of Jesus Christ.

Advent highlights and celebrates our desire and longing for peace, justice, and unity. The season helps us to see these deep longings in terms of Jesus' promise to return in glory and establish a new heaven and earth in which all people will be reconciled with God.

THE ADVENT WREATH

A wreath is often used in homes and schools during the Advent season as the focus of prayer.

The wreath is made of evergreen branches or boughs placed in a circle and four candles. The color of the candles is not the main issue. In some European countries the custom is four red candles. In North America, one tradition is to use three violet candles and one rose (for the third Sunday of Advent), corresponding to the color prescribed for the liturgical vestments worn by the priest or bishop at Mass. Four violet or white candles may also be used.

Each Sunday (Saturday evening), the beginning of a new week, the candles are lighted, reflecting the Sunday or week of Advent. The candles mark the steps in our Advent journey.

INTRODUCTION

The family gathers around the Advent wreath and lights the appropriate number of candles. If it is the first week, no candles are lit at this point. The candle corresponding to the Sunday of Advent will be lit before the intercessions.

All make the sign of the cross, as the leader says:

Leader: In the name of the Father, and of the Son, ✠
and of the Holy Spirit.

All: Amen.

The leader may add the following:

Leader: Our help is in the name of the Lord,

All: who made heaven and earth.

The leader may introduce the celebration, using these or similar words.

Leader: During Advent we wait in joyful hope
for the coming of our Lord Jesus Christ in glory.
Today we pray that God will (bless this wreath,)
keep us watchful in prayer,
and make us witnesses to Jesus,
the Lord of light and love,
who has taken on our human flesh
to bring salvation to all people.

Scripture Reading

Leader: Let us listen to these words of Scripture.

First Sunday (week)

Reader: The people who walked in darkness
have seen a great light;
those who lived in a land of deep darkness –
on them light has shined.
You have multiplied the nation,
you have increased its joy;
they rejoice before you as with joy at the harvest.
For a child has been born for us,
a son given to us;
authority rests upon his shoulders;
and he is named Wonderful Counselor,
Mighty God, Everlasting Father, Prince of Peace.

Isaiah 9.2b-3, 6.

Or:

Other Passages:

| James | 5.7-10 *the coming of the Lord;* |
| Matthew | 11.2-11 *are you the one who is to come?* |

A period of silence may be observed after the reading.

Second Sunday (week)

Reader: A shoot shall come out from the stump of Jesse,
and a branch shall grow out of his roots.
The spirit of the Lord shall rest on him,
the spirit of wisdom and understanding,
the spirit of counsel and might,
the spirit of knowledge and the fear of the Lord.
His delight shall be in the fear of the Lord.

Isaiah 11.1-3

Or:

Advent and Christmas

Other Passages:

1 Corinthians 1.3-9 *you wait for our Lord Jesus Christ;*
Mark   1.1-8 *the proclamation of John the Baptist.*

A period of silence may be observed after the reading.

Third Sunday (week)

Reader: They shall see the glory of the Lord,
    the majesty of our God.
    Then the eyes of the blind shall be opened,
    and the ears of the deaf unstopped;
    then the lame shall leap like the deer
    and the tongue of the speechless sing for joy.

    Isaiah 35.2c, 5-6a.

    Or:

Other Passages:

2 Peter 3.8-15 *the day of the Lord will come like a thief;*
Luke   1.26-38 *the Annunciation.*

A period of silence may be observed after the reading.

Fourth Sunday (week)

Reader: The Lord spoke to Ahaz, saying,
    Ask a sign of the Lord your God;
    let it be deep as Sheol or high as heaven.

    But Ahaz said, I will not ask,
    I will not put the Lord to the test.

    Then Isaiah said:
    "Hear then, O house of David!
    Is it too little for you to weary mortals,
    that you weary my God also?
    Therefore the Lord himself will give you a sign.
    Look, the young woman is with child
    and shall bear a son,
    and shall name him Emmanuel."

    Isaiah 7.10-14

    Or:

Other Passages:

Philippians   4.4-7 *always be joyful in the Lord;*
Matthew   1.18-24 *Joseph adopts Jesus as his son.*

A period of silence may be observed after the reading.

Lighting of the Candle

One member of the family may light the candle corresponding to the Sunday. A familiar Advent song may be sung during the lighting of the candle unless the following child's prayer is used.

A Child's Prayer

Prayer while lighting the Advent candle.

Child: O God,
as light comes from this candle,
may the blessing of Jesus Christ come to us,
warming our hearts
and brightening our way.
May Christ our Savior bring life
into the darkness of this world,
and to us, as we wait for his coming.

All: Amen.

INTERCESSIONS

Then leader invites all to pray.

Leader: Let us ask the Lord
to bless us with peaceful hope
as we gather in prayer.

All: R. Come, Lord Jesus, come.

Another person may announce the intentions.

Reader: Lord Jesus, light of the world:
come and make us your messengers. R.

Lord Jesus, giver of the Holy Spirit:
come and fill your people with love. R.

Lord Jesus, conqueror of darkness and sin:
come and shine your light upon us. R.

Lord Jesus, joy of the nations:
come and make us joyful in faith and hope. R.

Lord Jesus, prince of peace:
come and free us from fear and hatred. R.

Lord Jesus, source of endless life:
come and unite all people in God's kingdom. R.

Lord Jesus, good news of salvation:
come and keep us safe in your love. R.

Lord Jesus, enthroned in glory:
come and keep us watchful in prayer. R.

PRAYER OF PRAISE

The leader then says one of the following prayers.

On the First Sunday of Advent

Leader: God of hope and love,
we praise you for sending Jesus, your Son,
to save us from our sins
and to be the light in our darkness.
Bless us as we gather in his name,
and bless this wreath as a sign of your unending love
and of Jesus' presence among us.
Keep us watchful in prayer
as we await his return in glory.

We ask this through Jesus Christ our Lord,
who lives with you and the Holy Spirit,
in eternal glory,
one God, for ever and ever.

All: Amen.

On the Other Sundays and Weekdays of Advent

Leader: God of light and hope,
look upon us in love,
and fill us with the Spirit of Jesus
that we may love you and serve you in your kingdom.
Protect us during this week
and keep us watchful in prayer
as we await the coming of our Lord, Jesus Christ,
who is the light of the world,
and who lives and reigns with you and the Holy Spirit,
one God, for ever and ever.

All: Amen.

Or:

Leader: Almighty God,
strengthen the resolve of your faithful people
to prepare for the coming of your Christ
by works of justice and mercy,
so that when we go forth to meet him
he may call us to sit at his right hand
and possess the kingdom of heaven.

We ask this through our Lord Jesus Christ, your Son,
who lives and reigns with you
in the unity of the Holy Spirit,
God, for ever and ever.

All: Amen.

CONCLUSION

The leader may conclude with the following:

Leader: May Jesus Christ, coming in glory,
overcome the darkness of sin and sorrow.

All: Amen.

MEAL PRAYERS

The two proposed forms, *Before the Meal* and *After the Meal,* may be used in the same meal throughout Advent. If it is more convenient, one of the two could be used.

BEFORE THE MEAL

INTRODUCTION

Together, all make the sign of the cross.

Leader: In the name of the Father, and of the Son, ✠ and of the Holy Spirit.

All: Amen.

SCRIPTURE READING

The reader proclaims one of the following readings. Following the reading, the leader may say a few words on the meaning of the season of Advent and on our commitment to welcome Christ in our daily life, being challenged by his teaching of love and forgiveness.

Leader: Let us listen to these words from Scripture.

Reader: Let me hear what God the Lord will speak,
for he will speak peace to his people,
to his faithful, to those who turn to him in their hearts.
Surely his salvation is at hand for those who fear him,
that his glory may dwell in our land.

Psalm 85.8-9

Or:

Reader: Trust in the Lord forever,
for in the Lord God
you have an everlasting rock.
For he has brought low
the inhabitants of the height;
the lofty city he lays low.
He lays it low to the ground,
casts it to the dust.
The foot tramples it,
the feet of the poor,
the steps of the needy.

Isaiah 26.4-6

Or:

Reader: Jesus said to the Syrophoenician woman,
(who asked for her daughter to be healed)
"Let the children be fed first,
for it is not fair to take the children's food
and throw it to the dogs."
But she answered him,
"Sir, even the dogs under the table
eat the children's crumbs."

cf. *Mark 7.26-28*

Or:

Reader: The angel Gabriel came to Mary and said,
"Hail, full of grace!
The Lord is with you.
Do not be afraid, Mary,
for you have found favor with God.
And now, you will conceive in your womb
and bear a son, and you will name him Jesus.
He will be great,
and will be called the Son of the Most High,
And the Lord God will give to him
the throne of his ancestor David."
Then Mary said, "Here am I, the servant of the Lord;
let it be with me according to your word."

cf. *Luke* 1.28, 30-32, 38

Or:

Reader: John the Baptist
went into all the region around the Jordan,
proclaiming a baptism of repentance
for the forgiveness of sins,
as it is written in the book of the words
of the prophet Isaiah,
"The voice of one crying out in the wilderness:
'Prepare the way of the Lord, make his paths straight,
Every valley shall be filled,
and every mountain and hill shall be made low,
and the crooked shall be made straight,
and the rough ways made smooth;
and all flesh shall see the salvation of God.'"

cf. *Luke* 3.3-6

Or:

Reader: When Christ came into the world, he said,
"Sacrifices and offerings you have not desired,
but a body you have prepared for me;
in burnt offerings and sin offerings
you have taken no pleasure.
Then I said,
As it is written of me in the scroll of the book,
'See, God, I have come to do your will, O God.'"

Hebrews 10.5-7

LITANY

These litanies are optional.

The leader continues.

Leader: Let us ask the Lord to bless us with joyful hope as we gather in prayer.

All: R. Come, Lord Jesus, come.
        or: Come, Lord Jesus.

All pause for a moment of silent prayer.

Another person may announce the intentions:

Reader: Lord Jesus, light of the world,
come and make us your messengers. *R.*

Lord Jesus, giver of the Holy Spirit:
come and fill your people with love. *R.*

Lord Jesus, conqueror of darkness and sin:
come and shine your light upon us. *R.*

Lord Jesus, joy of the nations:
come and make us joyful in faith and hope. *R.*

Lord Jesus, prince of peace:
come and free us from fear and hatred. *R.*

Lord Jesus, source of endless life:
come and unite all people in God's kingdom. *R.*

Lord Jesus, good news of salvation:
come and keep us safe in your love. *R.*

Lord Jesus, enthroned in glory:
come and keep us watchful in prayer. *R.*

Or:

All: R. Come, Lord Jesus, come.
        or: Come, Lord Jesus.

Reader: Lord Jesus, you are the light of the world. R.

        You are light in our darkness. R.

        Son of God, save us from our sins. R.

        Bring hope into the lives of all people. R.

        Give your peace to all nations. R.

        Be the joy of all who love you. R.

        Bless us as we gather here in your name. R.

        Lord Jesus, stay with us. R.

THE LORD'S PRAYER

The leader invites all to recite the Lord's Prayer by saying:

Leader: We pray with Jesus, the prince of peace, our brother:

All: Our Father....

BLESSING

Leader: God, the Father of mercies,
        you willed your Son to take flesh,
        in order to give life back to us.
        Bless these your gifts
        with which we are about to nourish our bodies,
        so that, receiving new strength,
        we may wait in watchfulness
        for the glorious coming of Christ.
        who lives and reigns with you,
        in the unity of the Holy Spirit,
        one God, for ever and ever.

All: Amen.

Or, from December 17-24:

Leader: God of tenderness and love,
through the fruitful womb of the Virgin Mary
you fulfilled the expectation of the poor:
bless us abundantly
and grant us the same faith of Mary
so that we may welcome your Son in every person
and share our meal with the most needy.

We ask this through Christ our Lord.

All: Amen.

AFTER THE MEAL

RESPONSORY

Leader: Let us live soberly, justly, and devoutly in this world,

All: as we wait in joyful hope for the coming of our Savior, Jesus Christ.

Or:

Leader: Prepare the way of the Lord, make his paths straight.

All: All people shall see the salvation of God.

Or, from December 17-24:

Leader: Look, the virgin shall conceive and bear a son,

All: and they shall name him Emmanuel: God is with us.

Or, all may sing an appropriate Advent refrain.

Concluding Prayer

Leader: We give you thanks, Lord, God of hope,
for the gifts of your love;
as you nourish our body
and awaken us to your coming,
grant us to bend our angers into your peace,
to work for the good of our neighbor,
and to walk in your ways,
for ever and ever.

All: Amen.

CHRISTMAS SEASON

The Christmas season celebrates the mystery of the incarnation and the manifestation of Jesus Christ to the world (past, present and future). The Church does not merely remember historical events; it celebrates the enduring, ever-present mystery of the Word-made-flesh as we wait in blessed hope for the manifestation of the glory of our Savior, Jesus Christ. (see *Titus* 2.13)

The birth of Jesus begins the events that culminate in the events of his death and resurrection – the paschal mystery. The liturgy already looks forward to Easter: "He has come to raise the fallen world to himself, to make creation whole again, and to lead humanity from exile back to your heavenly kingdom." (Christmas Preface II)

The splendor and radiant glory of the Word-made-flesh makes Christmas a great festival of light. Jesus is the Light of the world who banishes the darkness. Coinciding with the winter solstice and the return of the sun, Christmas reveals Christ as the true and everlasting Light.

The mystery of the Word-made-flesh reveals the marvelous exchange that is God's plan for our salvation: as Christ shares in our humanity, we are called to share in his divinity. This exchange is a prominent feature of the Christmas season: "When your eternal Word assumes human frailty, our mortal nature takes on immortal value." (Christmas Preface III)

The season of Christmas begins with evening prayer on Christmas Eve and concludes with the feast of the Baptism of the Lord.

The season is marked by the many feasts of Christmas: Mary, the Mother of God, the Epiphany of the Lord, and the Baptism of the Lord. The Sunday within the octave of Christmas is celebrated as the feast of the Holy Family.

The Christmas season also contains the two holy days of obligation: the Birth of Christ (December 25) and the Solemnity of Mary, the Mother of God (January 1).

Family plans should ensure the importance of December 25 as the day on which the universal Church celebrates the Nativity of the Lord. The Christmas crib may be set up to focus the attention of the family on the centrality of the birth of Christ.

Families should avoid placing too much emphasis on or seeing the Christmas event exclusively as a past event. This fails to recognize the presence of Christ among us today or the action of God in our midst.

CHRISTMAS TREE

One legend regarding the first Christmas tree says an evergreen (a young fir tree) sprang from the center of an oak cut down by St. Boniface (ca. 675-754), who converted the German people to Christianity. The oak symbolized paganism, and its death brought an end to the old ways. The new tree was to be "the sign of endless life, for its leaves are evergreen." St. Boniface took this as a sign of the Christian faith.

The Christmas tree probably originated from popular early medieval religious plays. During Advent in the 11th century, popular religious plays called "mysteries" – including one about Paradise – were performed in churches and town squares of Europe. These mysteries told the story of the human race from the creation of Adam and Eve in the Garden of Paradise till the Birth of Jesus in Bethlehem. On stage was a great tree decorated with red apples which symbolized the Tree of Paradise. During the 15th century, the faithful began to put up a "paradise tree" laden with gifts and lighted with candles in their homes on December 24, the feast day of Adam and Eve. By the middle of the 16th century, decorated standing trees became popular in Germany and France.

The Christmas tree was introduced to America around 1700 by German immigrants, but the custom was not popular until the middle of the 19th century. The Christmas tree was introduced to Canada around the end of the 18th century even before it became a common practice in England.

The inauguration of the Christmas tree "offers an opportunity for family prayer. Apart from its historical origins, the Christmas tree has become a potent symbol today and is very diffuse among Christians; it evokes both the tree planted in the centre of Eden (Genesis 2.9), and the tree of the Cross, which lends it a Christological significance: Christ is the true tree of life, born of human stock, of the Virgin Mary, the tree which is always green and productive. In the Nordic countries, the tree is decorated with apples and hosts. 'Gifts' can be added; but among the gifts placed under the tree, something should be included for the poor, since they belong to every Christian family." (Directory on popular piety and the Liturgy, n. 109)

After the tree has been decorated with lights and some Christian symbols, the family gathers around it. Friends and neighbors may be invited for the lighting of the tree and the prayer service.

INTRODUCTION

All may sing a Christmas hymn or carol.

The leader may begin with the following.

Leader: All peoples have seen a great light.

All: The Lord has visited his people.

Or:

Leader: Glory to God in the highest.

All: And peace to God's people on earth.

SCRIPTURE READING

Leader: Let us listen to these words from Scriptures.

Reader: In the beginning was the Word,
and the Word was with God,
and the Word was God.
He was in the beginning with God.
All things came into being through him,
and without him not one thing came into being.
What has come into being in him was life,
and the life was the light of all people.
The light shines in the darkness
and the darkness did not overcome it.

John 1.1-5

Or:

Reader: In the day that the Lord God made the earth
and the heavens,
when no plant of the field was yet in the earth
and no herb of the field had yet sprung up—
for the Lord God had not caused it to rain
upon the earth,
and there was no one to till the ground—
then the Lord God formed man
from the dust of the ground,
and breathed into his nostrils the breath of life;
and the man became a living being.

And the Lord God planted a garden in Eden, in the east;
and there he put the man whom he had formed.

Out of the ground the Lord God made to grow every tree
that is pleasant to the sight and good for food,
the tree of life also in the midst of the garden.

Genesis 2.4-9

Or:

Reader: The true light, which enlightens everyone,
was coming into the world.
And the Word became flesh and lived among us,
and we have seen his glory,
the glory as of a father's only son,
full of grace and truth.
From his fullness we have all received,
grace upon grace.
The law indeed was given through Moses;
grace and truth came through Jesus Christ.
No one has ever seen God.
It is God the only Son,
who is close to the Father's heart,
who has made him known.

John 1.9,14,16-18

Or:

Other Passages:

Luke   2.1-14 *the birth of Jesus;* or 2.15-20 *the visit of the shepherds;* 2.25-32 *Simeon recognizes the Messiah in Jesus presented in the temple.*

After the reading all may pause for a moment of silent reflection on God's love for us. Then all may sing a verse of Christmas hymn or carol.

LITANY

The leader invites all to pray.

Leader: Let us praise God for the gift of love that is revealed in the birth of Jesus.

All: *R.* Blessed be God for ever.

Another person may read the intentions.

Reader: Blessed are you, Lord God of salvation. *R.*

Blessed is your holy name. *R.*

Blessed is your mercy and forgiveness. *R.*

Blessed is Jesus, who came to be one of us. *R.*

Blessed is Jesus, the light of the world. *R.*

Blessed is Jesus, the Savior of the nations. *R.*

Blessed is the Spirit of your love. *R.*

Blessed is the Spirit who makes us your children. *R.*

Blessed are you, Father, Son, and Holy Spirit. *R.*

Prayer of Praise

The leader adds the following prayer. All should stand.

Leader: All glory and praise to you,
Father of our Lord Jesus Christ,
for sending your Son in human flesh.
He became one of us
in order to make us your children,
and he died upon the tree of the cross
to bring us eternal life.

We praise you for the beauty of this tree
that we have decorated:
may its ever-green branches
remind us of your unending care for all people;
may its lights
illumine the darkness of the winter nights;
may its presence bring cheer and hope for all people.

As we gather in the presence of your Son,
we ask you to strengthen your love
in our family (and friends)
and grant that we may always rejoice
in the gift of salvation Jesus has given us.

Glory and praise to you, almighty God,
through Jesus Christ our Lord for ever and ever.

All: Amen.

Conclusion

All may share a sign of peace and sing a Christmas hymn or carol.

CHRISTMAS CRIB

The Christ Child in the manger and other pictures of the story of Bethlehem have been used in church services from the first centuries. But the *Christmas Crib* (or *Manger* or *Nativity scene* – or French, *crèche*) in its present form and its use outside the church originated with St. Francis of Assisi (1181/1182-1226): "I wish to recall to memory the little child who was born in Bethlehem, I want to set before our bodily eyes the hardship of his infant needs, how he lay in the manger, how with an ox and ass standing by he lay upon the hay." Through Francis' famous celebration at Greccio, Italy, on Christmas Eve, 1223, with a Bethlehem scene including live animals, he made the crib popular. Since then it has been a familiar sight in Christian homes all over the world.

Setting up the manger figures is a favorite family activity. Children like to arrange the figures of Mary and Joseph in the stable, and the shepherds, animals and other figures who are moved closer to the stable each day in anticipation of the arrival of the Christ Child. In many families, the figure of the Baby Jesus remains hidden until Christmas morning, when the children "discover" him in the manger. It is also a custom to have the figures of the wise men begin their approach towards Bethlehem on Christmas Day after the star has appeared, to arrive at the stable on the Epiphany.

The animals are traditionally part of every Nativity scene, although an ass and an ox are not mentioned in the New Testament. However, as early as the 4th century these animals were represented in pictures of the Nativity. The tradition originates in two Old Testament passages foretelling the birth of Christ: Isaiah 1.3 "The ox knows its owner, and the donkey its master's crib, but Israel does not know, my people do not understand"; and Habakkuk 3.2 (Septuagint version), "In the midst of two animals Thou shalt become known."

"'Live cribs' and the inauguration of the crib in the homes of the faithful is an opportunity for family prayer. This prayer should include a reading of St. Luke's account of the birth of Christ, the typical Christmas carols, as well as prayers of petition and praise, especially those of children who are the protagonists in such family moments."

(Directory on popular piety and the Liturgy, n. 109)

Close to the celebration of Christmas, after the crib has been set up in a special place (and the house or room or tree has been decorated), all may gather around the crib to bless and praise God for sending his Son, Jesus.

INTRODUCTION

All may sing a Christmas hymn or carol.

The leader may use the following antiphon to begin:

Leader: All the ends of the earth have seen,

All: the saving power of God.

Or:

Leader: Glory to God in the highest.

All: And peace to God's people on earth.

SCRIPTURE READING

The leader may invite all to listen to the story of Christmas by saying:

Leader: Let us listen to these words of Scripture.

A member of the family may read the following text.

Reader: Long ago God spoke to our ancestors in many and
various ways by the prophets,
but in these last days he has spoken to us by a Son,
whom he appointed heir of all things,
through whom he also created the worlds.
He is the reflection of God's glory
and the exact imprint of God's very being,
and he sustains all things by his powerful word.
Hebrews 1.1-3a

Or:

Reader: The grace of God has appeared,
bringing salvation to all,
training us to renounce impiety and worldly passions,
and in the present age to live lives
that are self-controlled, upright, and godly,
while we wait for the blessed hope
and the manifestation of the glory
of our great God and savior, Jesus Christ.

It is he who gave himself for us
that he might redeem us from all iniquity
and purify for himself a people of his own
who are zealous for good deeds.

Titus 2.11-14

Or:

Other Passages:

John 3.16-17 *God's love for us;*

Luke 1.28-33 *our Savior is coming;* or 2.1-5 *Bethlehem;* or 2.6-7 *birth of Jesus;* or 2.8-20 *shepherds.*

After the reading, all may reflect in silent prayer.

LITANY

The leader invites all to pray.

Leader: Let us praise our Lord Jesus Christ, the Savior of the world, who was born for our salvation.

All: R. Glory to God in the highest.

Another person may read the intentions.

Reader: Eternal Word,
you have scattered the darkness of sin and death. R.

Word made flesh,
you have made us children of God most high. R.

Incarnate Son,
you have united heaven and earth. R.

Lord Jesus,
you are the revelation of God's love. R.

Eternal Son,
you are the light of the nations. R.

Emmanuel,
you are fullness of God's glory. R.

Son of God,
you were born of Mary
with Joseph as your protector. R.

Bread of life,
you were laid in a humble manger. R.

Son of David,
the shepherds came to worship you. R.

Light of the world,
the Magi brought you gifts. R.

PRAYER OF PRAISE

The leader concludes the intercessions with the following prayer.

Leader: Blessed are you, Lord God of all creation:
you have sent your Son
as the promised Savior of the world
so that he might share with us your divine life.
Bless us as we prepare this crib,
and let it be a reminder of the Lord Jesus,
who was born of the Virgin Mary in the City of David.
Grant that we may always serve you in faith
as did the angels,
praise you for your saving deeds
as did the shepherds,
and surround you with the warmth of our love,
as did the animals of the stable.

Glory and praise to you, eternal God,
through Jesus Christ our Savior,
who lives with you and the Holy Spirit,
for ever and ever.

All: Amen.

CONCLUSION

The celebration may conclude with a Christmas hymn or carol (for example:
O come, all ye faithful) as all gather around the crib.

MEAL PRAYERS

It's Christmas, and so we celebrate the birth of Jesus, the Word made flesh, the Bread of Life. Jesus will feed crowds (see *John* 6.1-14) of people and say, "I am the Bread of life that comes down from heaven. The one who eats this bread will live forever" (*John* 6.48, 51, 58). In the Last Supper, he'll take a loaf of bread, break it and give it to his disciples, saying, "This is my body, which will be given up for you." (see *Luke* 22.19)

Jesus was born in Bethlehem, the city of David in the land of Judah. Since the name Bethlehem means "house of the bread", it is especially meaningful that Jesus, the Bread of life, was born in Bethlehem. Scripture tells us about the Magi finding the child Jesus laying in a manger (a stall or crib for feeding cattle), but the meaning of the manger becomes profound when we realize that it would be we who would eat the Bread of Life found within this humble "food container."

As we gather for this meal, we remember the One who nourishes our life and gives sense to it, Jesus, the Bread of Life.

During the Christmas season (December 25 through the Baptism of the Lord), the following may be used with, or in place of, the usual meal prayers. It may also be prayed at any gathering throughout Christmas.

It would be appropriate to have a candle lighted on the table.

The two proposed forms, *Before the Meal* and *After the Meal*, may be used in the same meal. If it is more convenient, one of the two could be used.

Before the Meal

Introduction

Together, all make the sign of the cross.

Leader: In the name of the Father, and of the Son, ✠
and of the Holy Spirit.

All: Amen.

Scripture Reading

The reader proclaims one of the following readings.

Following the reading, the leader may say a few words on the topic of Christmas season and on our life commitment to recognize the presence of Christ – the Emmanuel, the God with us – and to welcome him.

Leader: Let us listen to these words from Scripture.

Reader: On entering the house,
the wise men come from the East
saw the child with Mary his mother;
and they knelt down and paid him homage.
Then, opening their treasure chests,
they offered him gifts of gold, frankincense, and myrrh.

Matthew 2.11

Or:

Reader: Joseph went
from the town of Nazareth in Galilee to Judea,
to the city of David called Bethlehem,
because he was descended from the house

and family of David.
He went to be registered with Mary,
to whom he was engaged
and who was expecting a child.
While they were there,
the time came for her to deliver her child.
And she gave birth to her firstborn son
and wrapped him in swaddling cloths,
and laid him in a manger,
because there was no place for them in the inn.

Luke 2.4-7

Or:

Reader: And the Word became flesh and lived among us,
and we have seen his glory,
the glory as of a father's only son,
full of grace and truth.

John 1.14

Or:

Reader: Jesus said,
"Very truly, I tell you,
it was not Moses who gave you the bread from heaven,
but it is my Father who gives you
the true bread from heaven.
For the bread of God
is that which comes down from heaven
and gives life to the world."
They said to him,
"Sir, give us this bread always."
Jesus said to them,
"I am the bread of life.
Whoever comes to me will never be hungry,
and whoever believes in me will never be thirsty."

John 6.32-35

Or:

Other Passages:

Isaiah   52.7, 9-10 *how beautiful on the mountains are the feet of the messenger of good news;*

Matthew   11.18-19 *eating and drinking;*

1 John   3.16-20 *the proof of his love: he laid down his life for us.*

LITANY

These litanies are optional.

Leader: Let us praise our Lord Jesus Christ,
the Savior of the world
who was born for our salvation.

All: R. Glory to God in the highest.

Another person may read the intentions.

Reader: Eternal Word,
you have scattered the darkness
of sin and death. R.

Word made flesh,
you have made us children of God most high. R.

Bread of life, you are the true food
that comes down from heaven. R.

Incarnate Son,
you have united heaven and earth. R.

Lord Jesus,
you are the revelation of God's love. R.

Eternal Son,
you are the light of the nations. R.

Emmanuel,
you are fullness of God's glory. R.

Son of God,
you were born of Mary
with Joseph as your protector. R.

Or:

Leader: Let us praise the Father who sent his Son to live among us and to bring us new life.

All: R. Blessed are you, Lord God.

Another person may read the intentions.

Reader: Holy is your name. R.

You love your people with deepest love. R.

You sent your Son to be one of us. R.

You sent your Son to save us from sin. R.

Great is your mercy for your people. R.

You fill your children with joy. R.

You call us to praise your name. R.

Look with love on your holy Church. R.

Send the Spirit of your Son into our hearts. R.

THE LORD'S PRAYER

The leader may invite all to recite the Lord's Prayer by saying:

Leader: We pray with Jesus, the Word made flesh, our brother:

All: Our Father....

BLESSING

Leader: Lord our God,
the coming of your Son brings joy to the whole world.
Fill us with your love,
and the hungry with good things.
Bless our table and home
and grant that the food we share
increase our eagerness to serve you in each other.
Glory to you, Lord,
in the wonder of your presence among us
for ever and ever.

All: Amen.

Or:

Leader: Blessed are you, Lord God.
Through the fruitful virginity of Mary
you fulfilled the long expectation
of the poor and oppressed.
Grant that with the same faith
with which Mary awaited the birth of her Son,
we may look for him in our brothers and sisters in need.

We ask this through Christ our Lord.

All: Amen.

Or, on January 1:

Leader: O God of ancient blessing,
your servant Mary pondered in her heart
the treasured words spoken about her Son,
our Savior Jesus Christ.
Bless us, as we gather in his name,
and prepare our hearts to receive his Spirit,
that our tongues may confess him Lord,
every day of this new year,
and for ever and ever.

All: Amen.

Or, from Epiphany to the Baptism of the Lord:

Leader: O God of light and peace,
whose glory, shining in the child of Bethlehem,
still draws the nations to yourself:
bless us abundantly
and dispel the darkness that shrouds our path,
that, like the wise men, we may come
to kneel before Christ in true worship,
offer him our hearts and souls,
and return from his presence to live as he has taught,
now and for ever and ever.

All: Amen.

After the Meal

Responsory

Leader: Glory to God in the highest,

All: and peace to his people on earth.

Or:

Leader: The Word was made flesh, alleluia.

All: And dwelt among us, alleluia.

Or:

Leader: The bread of God
is that which comes down from heaven.

All: And gives life to the world.

Or:

Leader: All the ends of the earth have seen,

All: the saving power of God.

Or, all may sing one of the typical Christmas carols.

Concluding Prayer

Leader: God of faithful love,
we thank you for all your gifts to us,
especially for the gift of Jesus,
your Son and our brother.
Pour out your Spirit on us
to guide and strengthen us
as we walk your way each day.

We ask this through Christ our Lord.

All: Amen.

Or, on January 1:

Leader: Through the intercession of Mary, Mother of God,
may the Lord bless you and keep you;
may his face shine upon you,
and be gracious to you;
may he lift up his countenance upon you,
and give you peace, for ever and ever.

All: Amen.

Or, from Epiphany to the Baptism of the Lord:

Leader: Merciful God,
be gracious to us
and make your face to shine upon us,
so that your ways may be known upon earth,
your saving power among all nations,
for ever and ever.

All: Amen.

BLESSING OF FAMILIES

In some places it is customary to bless families on New Year's Day; the following prayers may be used.

On the feast of the Holy Family, the Sunday after Christmas (or December 30 when Christmas falls on a Sunday), the following blessing of families or children may be celebrated.

This blessing may be adapted for use at other times during the year.

INTRODUCTION

The family gathers near or around the crib or manger scene.

All make the sign of the cross, as the leader says:

Leader: In the name of the Father, and of the Son, ✠ and of the Holy Spirit.

All: Amen.

The leader may add:

Leader: Jesus Christ is the Savior of the world.

All: Thanks be to God.

The leader may then introduce the celebration, using these or similar words.

Leader: Jesus Christ, the Son of God,
left his heavenly home
in order to be born in a human family.
He was conceived by the power of the Holy Spirit,
born of the Virgin Mary,
and watched over by Joseph of Nazareth.
Today we ask God to bless our family (and friends),
and make us more like Christ our Savior.

SCRIPTURE READING

One of the following passages is read.

Leader: Let us listen to these words from Scripture.

Reader: The Lord bless you and keep you;
the Lord make his face to shine upon you,
and be gracious to you;
the Lord lift up his countenance upon you,
and give you peace.

Numbers 6.24-26

Or:

Reader: The grace of God has appeared,
bringing salvation to all,
training us to renounce impiety and worldly passions,
and in the present age to live lives
that are self-controlled, upright, and godly,
while we wait for the blessed hope
and the manifestation of the glory
of our great God and savior, Jesus Christ.
He it is who gave himself for us
that he might redeem us from all iniquity
and purify for himself a people of his own
who are zealous for good deeds.

Titus 2.11-14

Or:

Reader: See what love the Father has given us,
that we should be called children of God;
and that is what we are.
The reason the world does not know us
is that it did not know him.
Beloved, we are God's children now;
what we will be has not yet been revealed.
What we do know is this:
when he is revealed,
we will be like him,
for we will see him as he is.

I John 3.1-2

Or:

Advent and Christmas

Other Passages:

Galatians   4.4-7 *sons of God;*
Colossians   3.12-21 *you are the chosen of God;*
Titus   3.4-7 *the kindness and love of God our Savior;*
Matthew   1.18-25 *Joseph adopts Jesus as his son;*
John   1.1-5, 9-14 *the Word became flesh.*

A short time of reflection may follow.

INTERCESSIONS

The leader invites all to join in the intercessions:

Leader: Let us pray for ourselves and all families, especially for all parents and children. *R.*

All: *R.* Lord, hear us.
         or: Lord, hear our prayer.

Another person may announce the intentions.

Reader: Lord God, bless all families. *R.*

Bless this house and all who live here. *R.*

Fill us with the light of Jesus. *R.*

Give us happiness and health. *R.*

Make us gentle
and loving members of your family. *R.*

Keep us faithful to your love. *R.*

Bless our pope, bishops, and pastor. *R.*

Give comfort to all in need. *R.*

Remember the sick and lonely. *R.*

Give us a concern for the poor. *R.*

Help us share our gifts with others. *R.*

PRAYER OF PRAISE

The members of the family may lay their hands on the shoulders or head of each other.

The leader concludes the intercessions with one of the following.

Leader: God in heaven,
with a mother's tender embrace
you love and nurture us;
with a father's strength
you save and protect us.
We praise you for showing this great love
in the birth of Jesus your Son.
He had compassion for the poor and needy,
comforted the sick,
and cried with those who mourned.
Out of love for us he died upon the cross,
but you raised him to new life
by the power of the Holy Spirit.

Look upon our family and keep us close to you.
Grant that we may be like Jesus
and support, comfort, and help one another.
Give us a love like Mary's
that we may nurture the presence of Jesus
in each other and in all your people.
Give us a faith like Joseph's
that we may care for one another
and help those in need.

We praise and bless you, Lord God,
through Jesus Christ in the power of the Holy Spirit,
now and always and for ever.

All: Amen.

For Children

Leader: Lord Jesus, our Savior and brother,
you welcomed the little ones who came for your blessing,
and called them the sons and daughters of God.
In your love embrace these (our) children
and bless them with the gifts of your Spirit.
Grant that they may grow
in wisdom and grace in your presence
and always be pleasing to you.

We praise your name, Jesus,
for you are Lord for ever and ever.

All: Amen.

CONCLUSION

All may say the Lord's Prayer.

The members of the family may lay hands on the shoulders or head of each other, or exchange a sign of peace.

Blessing God
during Lent
and Easter

LENTEN SEASON

During Lent, the Church prepares to celebrate the dying and rising of the Lord Jesus. It is also the time for preparation for baptism, for those who will be baptized at Easter and for all who will renew their baptismal promises at the Vigil and on Easter Day.

MEAL PRAYERS

The two proposed forms, *Before the Meal* and *After the Meal,* may be used in the same meal throughout Lenten season. If it is more convenient, one of the two could be used.

BEFORE THE MEAL

INTRODUCTION

Together, all make the sign of the cross.

Leader: In the name of the Father, and of the Son, ☩ and of the Holy Spirit.

All: Amen.

SCRIPTURE READING

The reader proclaims one of the following readings.

Following the reading, the leader may say a few words on the topic of Lent and on our life commitment to convert and to closely follow Christ, our Master.

Leader: Let us listen to these words from Scripture.

Reader: Remember the long way
that the Lord your God has led you
these forty years in the wilderness,
in order to humble you,
testing you to know what was in your heart,
whether or not you would keep his commandments.

He humbled you by letting you hunger,
then by feeding you with manna,
with which neither you
nor your ancestors were acquainted,
in order to make you understand
that one does not live by bread alone,
but by every word
that comes from the mouth of the Lord.

Deuteronomy 8.2-3

Or:

Reader: Prayer with fasting is good,
but better than both is almsgiving with righteousness.
A little with righteousness
is better than wealth with wrongdoing.
It is better to give alms than to lay up gold.

Tobit 12.8

Or:

Reader: Wash yourselves;
make yourselves clean;
remove the evil of your doings
from before my eyes;
cease to do evil,
learn to do good;
seek justice,
rescue the oppressed,
defend the orphan,
plead for the widow.

Isaiah 1.16-17

Or:

Reader: After being baptized,
Jesus was led up by the Spirit
into the wilderness to be tempted by the devil.
He fasted forty days and forty nights,
and afterwards he was famished.
The tempter came and said to him,
"If you are the Son of God,
command these stones to become loaves of bread."
But he answered, "It is written,
'One does not live by bread alone,
but by every word that comes from the mouth of God.'"

Matthew 4.1-4

Or:

Reader: Jesus said to the disciples,
"Whenever you fast,
do not look dismal, like the hypocrites,
for they disfigure their faces
so as to show others that they are fasting.
Truly I tell you, they have received their reward.
But when you fast,
put oil on your head and wash your face,
so that your fasting may be seen not by others
but by your Father who is in secret;
and your Father who sees in secret will reward you."

cf. *Matthew* 6.16-18

Or:

Reader: As Jesus sat at dinner in the house,
many tax collectors and sinners came
and were sitting with him and his disciples.
When the Pharisees saw this, they said to his disciples,
"Why does your teacher eat
with tax collectors and sinners?"
But when he heard this, he said,
"Those who are well have no need of a physician,
but those who are sick.
Go and learn what this means,
'I desire mercy, not sacrifice.'
For I have come to call not the righteous but sinners."

cf. *Matthew* 9.10-13

Or:

Reader: If anyone is in Christ,
there is a new creation:
everything old has passed away;
see, everything has become new!
All this is from God,
who reconciled us to himself through Christ,
and has given us the ministry of reconciliation;
that is,
in Christ God was reconciling the world to himself,
not counting their trespasses against them,
and entrusting the message of reconciliation to us.
So we are ambassadors for Christ,
since God is making his appeal through us;
we entreat you on behalf of Christ,
be reconciled to God.

2 Corinthians 5.17-20

LITANY

These litanies are optional.

Leader: Lord Jesus,
you came to save us from our sins.

All: *R.* Lord, have mercy.

Leader: You fasted to encourage us to do penance. *R.*

You suffered temptation to give us strength. *R.*

You were transfigured to give us hope. *R.*

You suffered insults to bring us salvation. *R.*

You accepted death to bring us life in you. *R.*

Other acclamations or petitions may be added.

Or:

Leader: Christ, our Lord,
you endured the agony in the garden
to strengthen us in prayer.

All: *R.* Christ, have mercy.

Leader: You carried your Cross to save us. *R.*

You were nailed to the Cross.
to heal our wounds of sin. *R.*

You died on the the Cross to bring us eternal life. *R.*

You were raised to life
so that we could live with you for God. *R.*

Or (see *Matthew* 25.35-36):

Leader: I was hungry,

All: and you gave me food.

Leader: I was thirsty,

All: and you gave me drink.

Leader: I was a stranger,

All: and you welcomed me.

Leader: I was naked,

All: and you clothed me.

Leader: I was ill,

All: and you comforted me.

Leader: I was in prison,

All: and you came to see me.

Other acclamations or prayers may be added.

THE LORD'S PRAYER

The leader invites all to recite the Lord's Prayer by saying:

Leader: We pray with Jesus, the beloved Son, our brother:

All: Our Father....

BLESSING

Leader: Lord Jesus Christ,
may our Lenten fasting turn us
toward all our brothers and sisters who are in need.
Bless this table, our good food, and ourselves.
Send us through Lent with good cheer,
and bring us to the fullness of your Passover,
now and for ever and ever.

All: Amen.

Or:

Leader: O God,
we hunger and thirst for you.
Bless us, as we gather at this table,
and fill our hearts with your love today.
May we praise you with joy
and serve you in our brothers and sisters.
We ask this through Christ our Lord.

All: Amen.

Or:

Leader: Blessed are you, Father,
for you have taught us
the fundamental commandment of love and forgiveness.
May the example of your Son, Jesus,
teach us to serve you and one another
and to be always thankful for the many gifts
we receive from you
through Christ our Lord.

All: Amen.

Or:

Leader: Lord Jesus,
in order to fulfill the will of the Father,
you became obedient to the point of death,
even death on a Cross,
bless us who are gathered at this table,
so that we may share the same spiritual food as you
and that we may feel
how good, benevolent, and perfect is the will of God,
for you live and reign for ever and ever.

All: Amen.

AFTER THE MEAL

RESPONSORY

Leader: No one lives by bread alone,

All: but by every word that comes from the mouth of God.

Or:

Leader: The Son of Man came not to be served but to serve,

All: and to give his life as a ransom for many.

Or, during Holy Week:

Leader: Christ became obedient to the point of death,

All: even death on a Cross.

Or, all may sing an appropriate Lenten refrain.

CONCLUDING PRAYER

Leader: Loving God,
help us to continue to die to sin
so that we may always live for you
with Christ our Lord.

All: Amen.

ALMS AND OFFERINGS

On days of fasting and abstinence, special effort should be made to cut down on the amount and variety of food (in comparison to an ordinary meal), so that the money saved may be given to the poor and needy. This money may be dedicated at this meal in the blessing prayer.

Concern for others in need may also be expressed by inviting someone – a pensioner, a person of limited means, a convalescing neighbor – to share in this meal, or by bringing a substantial meal (a good piece of meat, a special dessert) to such a person.

Ash Wednesday and Good Friday are days of fasting and abstinence from meat. Fridays are days of abstinence from meat, but we may perform special acts of charity or piety instead.

HOLY WEEK

During Holy Week the Church celebrates the paschal mystery: the events of our salvation accomplished by Christ in the last days of his life on earth. The week begins with Passion Sunday – the commemoration of Jesus' messianic entrance into Jerusalem. The liturgies of these days have precedence over all other celebrations.

"The days of his life-giving death and glorious resurrection are approaching. This is the hour when he triumphed over Satan's pride, the time when we celebrate the great event of our redemption." (Passion Preface II)

Palm Sunday

Passion (Palm) Sunday ushers in Holy Week, the final days of the Lenten season. Red vestments are worn on this Sunday, in keeping with the Church's focus on the Lord's glorious Passion.

The celebration begins with a commemoration of the Lord's entrance into Jerusalem. The parish community gathers in a place separate from the church, at the church entrance, or inside the church itself. The blessing of palms is followed by a festive procession. After the procession, Mass continues as usual.

The proclamation of the Passion is the centerpiece of the celebration. During the reading, the people signal their participation by standing and by taking part in the sung acclamations that are interspersed in the text.

Placing of the Palm Branch(es) in the Home

After the family returns from church, they may place the palm branch(es) in a place of honor, for example attached to a crucifix or icon.

The following prayer may be said.

Leader: Blessed are you, Lord our God,
creator of the universe and source of mercy and love,
you sent your Son in human flesh to be our king.

He proclaimed that your kingdom is near,
and taught that those who rule
must be servant of all.
He crowned his life, not with the glory of this world,
but by fulfilling your will
and offering his life for the salvation of the world.
On the third day you raised him in glory
and exalted him at your right hand.

Today we proudly carry
this (palm) branch in his honor,
and place it in our home
as a sign of his victory over sin and death.

May the presence of this (palm) branch
remind us of the glory of your kingdom
and inspire us to love and serve you in others.

Glory and praise to you, Lord God, for ever and ever.

All: Amen.

MEAL PRAYERS FOR HOLY WEEK

During the days of Holy Week, the following may be prayed with or in place of the usual meal prayers. They may also be used at any gathering or to begin or end a time of personal prayer.

BEFORE THE MEAL

INTRODUCTION

Together, all make the sign of the cross.

Leader: In the name of the Father, and of the Son, ✠ and of the Holy Spirit.

All: Amen.

SCRIPTURE READING

The reader proclaims one of the following readings.

Following the reading, the leader may say a few words on the topic of Lent and on our life commitment to convert and to closely follow Christ, our Master.

Leader: Let us listen to these words from Scripture.

Reader: Christ humbled himself
and became obedient to the point of death –
even death on a cross.
Therefore God also highly exalted him
and gave him the name
that is above every name.

Philippians 2.8-9

Or:

Reader: At the Last Supper,
Jesus took his place with the twelve;
and while they were eating, he said,
"Truly I tell you, one of you will betray me."
And they became greatly distressed
and began to say to him one after another,
"Surely not I, Lord?"
He answered,
"The one who has dipped his hand
into the bowl with me will betray me.
The Son of Man goes as it is written of him,
but woe to that one
by whom the Son of Man is betrayed!
It would have been better
for that one not to have been born."
Judas, who betrayed him,
said, "Surely not I, Rabbi?"
Jesus replied, "You have said so."

cf. *Matthew* 26.21-25

LITANY

Leader: Christ, our Lord,
you endured the agony in the garden
to strengthen us in prayer.

All: R. Holy is God!
Holy and strong!
Holy immortal one, have mercy on us.

or: Lord, have mercy.

Leader: You carried your Cross to save us. R.

You were nailed to the Cross.
to heal our wounds of sin. R.

You died on the Cross to bring us eternal life. R.

You were raised to life
so that we could live with you for God. R.

Lent and Easter

The Lord's Prayer

The leader invites all to recite the Lord's Prayer by saying:

Leader: We pray with Jesus, the suffering Servant, our brother:

All: Our Father....

Concluding Prayer

Leader: Saving God,
you sent your Son to us because you love us
and want to save us.
By the power of his Cross,
free us from sin
and let us live each day for you.

We ask this through Christ our Lord.

All: Amen.

After the Meal

Responsory

Leader: Christ became obedient to the point of death,

All: even death on a Cross.

Or:

Leader: Lord,
by your Cross and resurrection you have set us free,

All: you are the Savior of the world.

Or, all may sing an appropriate Lenten refrain.

Concluding Prayer

Leader: Merciful God, Father of all nations,
look kindly upon your family gathered here
who joyfully came to this table;
grant us to be with you and your Son, ‸
one day, in your kingdom,
sharing with you eternal joy,
for ever and ever.

All: Amen.

Paschal Fast

The Church of God fasts on Good Friday and continues in fasting and prayer on Holy Saturday. This honors the suffering and death of the Lord Jesus and prepares us to share more deeply in the joy of his resurrection.

Through the paschal fast, the people of God strive to receive the joys of Easter with uplifted and responsive hearts.

EASTER TRIDUUM

Through his paschal mystery the Lord Jesus redeemed humanity and gave perfect praise to the Father. By dying, Christ destroyed our death; by rising, he restored our life. For this reason the Easter "Triduum" is the high point of the Church year. These are the days when we remember and celebrate the suffering, death, and resurrection of the Lord. The Easter solemnity is to the year what Sunday is to the week.

The Triduum covers the period of Holy Thursday through Easter Sunday.

- It opens on Holy Thursday with the evening Mass of the Lord's Supper, the night Jesus was given up to death.

- On Good Friday the Church meditates on the Passion of the Lord, adores his Cross, and prays for the salvation of the world.*

- Holy Saturday finds the people of God in recollection at the Lord's tomb, meditating on his suffering and death. At the solemn Vigil service – the event that St. Augustine called the "mother of all vigils" – we gather in prayer to await the resurrection and to celebrate the sacraments of initiation.

- Sunday morning breaks forth in the full light of Easter. The Church celebrates the resurrection of the Lord with solemnity and joy. The Triduum ends with evening prayer on Easter night.

These should be days of special prayer and reflection in personal and family life.

---

* If for some reason, the family does not have the opportunity to attend the *Celebration of the Lord's Passion*, it may be appropriate to do the *Way of the Cross* (see pages 290-309).

EASTER SEASON

The Easter festival is an extended event. The fifty days from Easter to Pentecost Sunday are kept as one great feast day – called the "Great Sunday."

Certain signs in the church, liturgy, and prayers mark the season.

- The paschal candle stands near the altar or ambo as a sign of the presence of the risen one.

- The sacraments of initiation have a special place in these weeks. Parishes celebrate confirmation and first Communion.

- The Old Testament reading is replaced by passages from the Acts of the Apostles and the Book of Revelation.

- "*Alleluia*" is sung often in the liturgy as a sign of the Church's rejoicing.

- "*Regina Caeli*" (see page 316) is recited instead of the "*Angelus*" (see page 315) Marian Prayer.

The Easter season comes to its climax and close on the evening of Pentecost Sunday.

EASTER EGGS

The egg has been the most identifiable Easter symbol for centuries; it's the symbol of fertility and new life. Just as the chick breaks the bondage of its shell and emerges into new life, so too did our Savior when he broke the fetters of death and emerged from the rock tomb to give us everlasting life.

In many Old World countries fasting involved giving up dairy products as well as meat. On the Tuesday before Ash Wednesday the house was cleansed of all eggs, milk, and cheese. This led to the custom of Shrove or Pancake Tuesday.

Lent was springtime in these countries. Thus, the eggs were not eaten so that new chicks could be born. Milk (and therefore, cheese) was not available because it was needed for the calves and kid-goats. Animals could not be slaughtered for meat because they were needed to feed and care for their young.

This led to the custom of joyfully decorating, hunting, and eating eggs on Easter Sunday. Although eggs represent new life, the symbolism for Christians goes deeper – it represents the emergence of Christ from his tomb into everlasting life. That's why at Easter, they are decorated with symbols of Easter, *Alleluia,* and blessed along with other festive foods.

Leader: Almighty and everliving God,
on the fifth day of creation,
you made the birds to fly above the earth.
As we see them multiplying on the earth,
we recognize in their breaking the shell at birth,
a symbol of the raising up of our Lord Jesus Christ
who came forth from the rock tomb,
a sign of the emergence of a new life.

Look with favor on these decorated eggs
that we are going to share on this Easter day,
in which you made all things new,
bestow your blessing upon them,
so that we, who are reborn in Baptism,
may break and eat them
in joyful celebration of the Resurrection of your Son,
who lives and reigns with you for ever and ever.

All: Amen.

BLESSING OF FESTIVE FOODS

It is the tradition in many cultures for people to ask for God's blessing on the festive foods to be used at Easter.

When the Vigil was celebrated on Holy Saturday morning, the blessing of food followed. Now that the Easter Vigil has been restored to the night hours, the blessing may be celebrated after the Vigil, on Easter Sunday, or later in the Easter season.

If a priest is not available, the following may be used at home.

At the end of the blessing, if water from the Easter Vigil is available, the leader may sprinkle it over the food and the people.

Leader: Lord Jesus Christ,
after you were raised from the dead
you prepared food on a charcoal fire,
and invited your disciples to come and have breakfast.

As we celebrate your resurrection,
come to our table:
open our eyes to your glorious presence,
our minds to the holy Scriptures,
and bless our food so that we may joyfully partake
in the sharing of the victory of your love over hatred
and life over death,
for ever and ever.

All: Amen.

See *John* 21.4-14; *Luke* 24.13-35

PRAYERS FOR THE SEASON OF EASTER

It is appropriate on Easter afternoon/evening and during Easter season to have a moment of prayer, inspired by the experience of the disciples of Emmaus:

1. To go on a walk together and to share about what we have experienced during the past days (Lenten season, Holy Week, Easter);

2. To read the gospel: *Luke* 24.13-35;

3. At meal, to share about the presence of the risen Christ in our lives.

4. To pray the following litany.

This litany may be used with, or in place of, the usual meal prayers during the Easter season. It may also be used at any gathering throughout the 50 days of Easter.

Leader: Jesus our risen Lord is always with us,
for we are God's beloved children.
Father of life, we praise you.

All: R.   Christ is risen, alleluia!
or: Alleluia!

Leader: You have given Jesus victory over sin. R.

You have raised him from the dead. R.

You have made his Cross a sign of glory. R.

You have made us sharers in your life. R.

With Christ you have buried us to sin. R.

With him you have raised us to new life. R.

Jesus is seated with you in glory. R.

He sends his Spirit to guide our lives. R.

He will come again in glory. R.

Other acclamations or petitions may be added.

Leader: We praise you, Lord,
for raising your Son Jesus from the dead
and for giving him victory over sin.
Make us holy as we follow him in love,
and fill us with your Spirit,
for ever and ever.

All: Amen.

Or, at evening:

Leader: O God, at this evening hour,
the risen Christ revealed himself to his disciples
in the breaking of bread.
Feed us with the bread of life
and break open our hearts,
that we may know him
not only in the good news of the Scriptures,
but risen in the midst of your pilgrim people,
now and for ever.

All: Amen.

MEAL PRAYERS

It would be appropriate to have an Easter candle lighted on the table.

The two proposed forms, *Before the Meal* and *After the Meal,* may be used in the same meal. If it is more convenient, one of the two could be used.

BEFORE THE MEAL

INTRODUCTION

Together, all make the sign of the cross.

Leader: In the name of the Father, and of the Son, ✠
and of the Holy Spirit.

All: Amen.

SCRIPTURE READING

The reader proclaims one of the following readings.

Following the reading, the leader may say a few words on the topic of Easter and on the new way of Jesus, the risen Lord, to be present to his disciples, to all people and families gathered in his name.

Leader: Let us listen to these words from Scripture.

Reader: As Jesus was walking with the disciples of Emmaus,
they came near the village to which they were going,
he walked ahead as if he were going on.
But they urged him strongly, saying,
"Stay with us, because it is almost evening
and the day is now nearly over." ➤

So he went in to stay with them.
When he was at the table with them,
he took bread, blessed and broke it,
and gave it to them.
Then their eyes were opened,
and they recognized Jesus;
and he vanished from their sight.
The two disciples said to each other,
"Were not our hearts burning within us
while he was talking to us on the road,
while he was opening the scriptures to us?"

cf. *Luke* 24.28-32

Or:

Reader: When the disciples had gone ashore,
they saw a charcoal fire there,
with fish on it, and bread.
Jesus said to them,
"Bring some of the fish that you have just caught."
So Simon Peter went aboard
and hauled the net ashore, full of large fish,
a hundred fifty-three of them;
and though there were so many,
the net was not torn.
Jesus said to them, "Come and have breakfast."
Now none of the disciples dared to ask him,
"Who are you?"
because they knew it was the Lord.
Jesus came and took the bread and gave it to them,
and did the same with the fish.
This was now the third time
that Jesus appeared to the disciples
after he was raised from the dead.

John 21.9-14

Or:

Lent and Easter

Reader: All who believed were together
and had all things in common;
they would sell their possessions and goods
and distribute the proceeds to all, as any had need.
Day by day,
as they spent much time together in the temple,
they broke bread at home
and ate their food with glad and generous hearts,
praising God and having the goodwill of all the people.

Acts 2.44-47

Or:

Reader: About noon the next day,
Peter went up on the roof to pray.
He became hungry and wanted something to eat;
and while it was being prepared, he fell into a trance.
He saw the heaven opened
and something like a large sheet coming down,
being lowered to the ground by its four corners.
In it were all kinds of four-footed creatures
and reptiles and birds of the air.
Then he heard a voice saying,
"Get up, Peter; kill and eat."
But Peter said, "By no means, Lord;
for I have never eaten anything
that is profane or unclean."
The voice said to him again, a second time,
"What God has made clean,
you must not call profane."

Acts 10.9-15

Or:

Reader: Blessed be the God
and Father of our Lord Jesus Christ!
By his great mercy
he has given us a new birth into a living hope
through the resurrection of Jesus Christ from the dead.
May grace and peace be yours in abundance.

1 Peter 1.3, 2

Or, from the Ascension to Pentecost:

Reader: On the last day of the festival, the great day,
while Jesus was standing there,
he cried out,
"Let anyone who is thirsty come to me,
and let the one who believes in me drink.
As the scripture has said,
'Out of the believer's heart
shall flow rivers of living water.'"
Now he said this about the Spirit,
which believers in him were to receive;
for as yet there was no Spirit,
because Jesus was not yet glorified.

John 7.37-39

It is appropriate to include a litany here (see page 269).

THE LORD'S PRAYER

The leader may invite all to recite the Lord's Prayer by saying:

Leader: We pray with Jesus, the risen Lord, our brother:

All: Our Father....

BLESSING

During the Octave of Easter (Easter Sunday to the Second Sunday of Easter):

Leader: After forty days of prayer and penance
we rejoice with the entire Church in the resurrection of
Jesus our Lord. Let us bow our heads in prayer, and
ask God to bless us.

After a moment of silent prayer, the leader continues:

Blessed are you, God of mercy and love:
you have guided us through prayer and fasting
to this feast of the resurrection.
Fill our celebration with joy and gladness,
that this food may be a sign of the heavenly banquet.
Bless our gathering and this food (or N.)
that we may always live the new life of baptism,
won for us by Jesus Christ, our risen Lord,
who is exalted at your right hand,
reigning in eternal splendor, for ever and ever.

All: Amen.

During the Easter season (Second Sunday of Easter to Pentecost):

Leader: We joyfully sing your praises, Lord Jesus Christ,
who on the day of your resurrection
was recognized by your disciples
in the breaking of the bread.
Remain here with us
as we gratefully partake of these gifts
and bless our table;
teach us to welcome you as a guest
in our brothers and sisters,
and welcome us on the last Day
at the banquet table in your Kingdom,
where you live and reign for ever and ever.

All: Amen.

After the Meal

Responsory

Leader: Christ is risen, alleluia!

All: Truly he is risen, alleluia!

Or:

Leader: This is the day the Lord has made,

All: let us rejoice and be glad.

Or:

Leader: The disciples recognized the Lord, alleluia.

All: In the breaking of the bread, alleluia.

During, from Ascension to Pentecost:

Leader: Lord, send out your Spirit,

All: and renew the face of the earth.

Or, all may sing an appropriate Easter refrain.

Concluding Prayer

Leader: God, source of life,
pour in our hearts the joy of Easter,
you who fed us by the fruits of the earth,
and grant us to live the new life
that Christ has gained for us through his resurrection,
for he reigns with you, in the unity of the Holy Spirit,
one God for ever and ever.

All: Amen.

PENTECOST

During the days between Ascension and Pentecost, the Church prays for the gifts of the Holy Spirit.

These are the days of the original novena prayer.

The following may be prayed with the usual meal prayers, at any gathering, or to begin or end a time of personal prayer.

Leader: Blessed are you, Lord God,
you have forgiven us our sins
and called us to be your holy people.
Give us your Spirit to guide us each day,
so that we may continue to die to sin
and to live with Jesus for you.

We ask this grace
through Jesus, our Lord and brother,
in the communion of your Holy Spirit.

All: Amen.

Or:

Leader: Lord Jesus,
send your Spirit into our hearts
so that we may die to sin
and live with you for the Father's glory,
now and for ever.

All: Amen.

Or:

Leader: God of majesty,
you sent the Holy Spirit upon your apostles
as they were joined in prayer with Mary,
the mother of Jesus;
grant through her intercession
that we may serve you faithfully
and, by word and example,
spread the glory of your name throughout the world.

We ask this through Christ our Lord.

All: Amen.

For other prayers associated with confirmation, see pages 73-78, or 287.

Praying
with Traditional
and Common Words

Sign of the Cross

The sign of the cross is not only an action, but a statement of faith itself. In this simple gesture one makes a sign of our redemption, the Cross, and expresses faith in the Blessed Trinity. This is the first sign that we receive as, through baptism, we become members of the Church, according to the words of Jesus: "Go therefore and make disciples of all nations, baptizing them in the name of the Father and of the Son and of the Holy Spirit." (*Matthew* 28, 19)

> In the name of the Father, and of the Son, ✠
> and of the Holy Spirit. Amen.

The Lord's Prayer

This prayer was given to us by our Lord Jesus Christ himself when the apostles asked him to teach them how to pray (cf. *Luke* 11.1-4, *Matthew* 6.9-13). Thus it has been a part of the Church since the very beginning. The *Didache* (1st–2nd century) commends the prayer to be recited by the faithful three times during the day. In the latter part of the 4th century it became an official part of the Eucharist.

> Our Father, who art in heaven,
> hallowed be thy name;
> thy kingdom come,
> thy will be done,
> on earth as it is in heaven.
> Give us this day our daily bread;
> and forgive us our trespasses
> as we forgive those who trespass against us;
> and lead us not into temptation,
> but deliver us from evil.

Traditional and Common Prayers

Modern Text*

Our Father in heaven,
hallowed be your name,
your kingdom come,
your will be done,
on earth as in heaven.
Give us today our daily bread.
Forgive us our sins
as we forgive those who sin against us.
Save us in the time of trial,
and deliver us from evil.

For the kingdom, the power, and the glory are yours
now and for ever.

DOXOLOGY

The Doxology is a short expression of praise to the Trinity from the very early Church.
Authors such as Hippolytus (170-236) and Origen (c.185-254) use very similar phrases
in praise of the Trinity. The current form was fixed by the time of the Arian controversies
of the 4th century. It is used extensively in the Liturgy of the Hours and also many other
devotions, such as the Rosary.

Glory be to the Father, and to the Son,
and to the Holy Spirit.
As it was in the beginning, is now, and ever shall be,
world without end. Amen.

Modern Text

Glory to the Father, the Son, and the Holy Sprit:
as it was in the beginning,
is now, and will be for ever. Amen.

* English translation of the Lord's Prayer by the International Consultation on English
Texts (ICET)

PROFESSION OF FAITH

APOSTLES' CREED

I believe in God, the Father almighty,
    creator of heaven and earth.

I believe in Jesus Christ, his only Son, our Lord.
    He was conceived by the power of the Holy Spirit
    and born of the Virgin Mary.
    He suffered under Pontius Pilate,
        was crucified, died, and was buried.
    He descended to the dead.
    On the third day he rose again.
    He ascended into heaven,
        and is seated at the right hand of the Father.
    He will come again in glory to judge the living and the dead.

I believe in the Holy Spirit,
    the holy catholic Church,
    the communion of saints,
    the forgiveness of sins,
    the resurrection of the body,
    and the life everlasting. Amen.

NICENE CREED

We believe in one God,
    the Father, the Almighty,
    maker of heaven and earth,
    of all that is seen and unseen.

We believe in one Lord, Jesus Christ,
    the only Son of God,
    eternally begotten of the Father.
    God from God, Light from Light,
    true God from true God,
    begotten, not made, one in Being with the Father.

Through him all things were made.
For us men and for our salvation
he came down from heaven:
by the power of the Holy Spirit
he was born of the Virgin Mary, and became man.
For our sake he was crucified under Pontius Pilate;
he suffered, died, and was buried.
On the third day he rose again
in fulfillment of the Scriptures;
he ascended into heaven
and is seated at the right hand of the Father.
He will come again in glory to judge the living and the dead,
and his kingdom will have no end.

We believe in the Holy Spirit, the Lord, the giver of life,
who proceeds from the Father and the Son.
With the Father and the Son he is worshipped and glorified.
He has spoken through the prophets.
We believe in one holy catholic and apostolic Church.
We acknowledge one baptism for the forgiveness of sins.
We look for the resurrection of the dead,
and the life of the world to come. Amen.

ACT OF CONTRITION

My God,
I am sorry for my sins with all my heart.
In choosing to do wrong and failing to do good,
I have sinned against you
whom I should love above all things.
I firmly intend, with your help,
to do penance, to sin no more,
and to avoid whatever leads me to sin.
Our Savior Jesus Christ suffered and died for us.
In his name, my God, have mercy.

ACTS OF THEOLOGICAL VIRTUES

The origin of the three theological virtues of faith, hope, and love lies with Scripture, in which they are constantly stressed. For example, in his letter to the Corinthians St. Paul writes: "And now faith, hope, and love abide, these three; and the greatest of these is love" (1 Corinthians 13.13). Since faith, hope and love are virtues that have God as proper and immediate object, they are called "theological virtues" ('theological' means 'belonging to or relating to God'). Our faith, hope, and love must have God for their basis and motive, otherwise they are worthless.

Different historical periods have emphasized different virtues. Augustine (354-430) saw love as the ordering virtue. Martin Luther (1483-1546) placed faith at the center of Christian life. Two popes in particular felt very strongly about the three theological virtues. Pope Benedict XIII (1649-1730), on January 15, 1728, granted a plenary indulgence to the acts of faith, hope, and love. Twenty-eight years later, on January 28, 1756, Pope Benedict XIV (1675-1758) confirmed his predecessor's grant and extended the grant to include a partial indulgence whenever they were recited. He also extended the grant to any legitimate forms of the three theological virtues. This later grant continues to today in the *Enchiridion Indulgentiarum*. A partial indulgence is granted to any legitimate act of faith, hope, or love.

There are many versions of these acts of faith, hope, and love. The ones given below are the popular ones seen these days, such as those found in the Baltimore Catechism.

ACT OF FAITH

"Without faith it is impossible to please God, for whoever would approach him must believe that he exists and that he rewards those who seek him." (*Hebrews* 11.6)

O my God, I firmly believe
that you are one God in three divine Persons,
Father, Son, and Holy Spirit.
I believe that your divine Son became man, died for our sins,
and that he will come to judge the living and the dead.
I believe these and all the truths
which the holy Catholic Church teaches,
because you have revealed them,
who can neither deceive nor be deceived.

ACT OF HOPE

"We ourselves, who have the first fruits of the Spirit, groan inwardly while we wait for adoption, the redemption of our bodies. For in hope we were saved." (*Romans* 8.23-24)

O my God,
relying on your almighty power and infinite mercy and promises,
I hope to obtain pardon of my sins,
the help of your grace,
and life everlasting
through the merits of Jesus Christ, my Lord and Redeemer.

ACT OF LOVE

"'You shall love the Lord your God with all your heart, and with all your soul, and with all your mind.' This is the greatest and first commandment. And a second is like it: 'You shall love your neighbor as yourself.'" (*Matthew* 22.37-39)

O my God, I love you above all things,
with my whole heart and soul,
because you are all good and worthy of all love.
I love my neighbor as myself for the love of you.
I forgive all who have injured me,
and ask pardon of all whom I have injured. Amen.

JESUS PRAYER

The *Jesus Prayer,* a favorite especially in the Eastern Churches, is a prayer that can be said sitting, kneeling, standing, walking, lying down – any way that seems good to the person praying it. It is repeated endlessly as a litany until it becomes part of one's heart. Some people repeat it up to 6,000 times a day. In order to track the number of repetitions, a prayer rope may be used.

Lord Jesus Christ, Son of the living God,
have mercy on me, a sinner.

It is recommended that this prayer accompany one's breath: as you breathe in, say "Lord Jesus Christ, Son of the living God," and as you breathe out, say "have mercy on me, a sinner."

PRAYER FOR PEACEMAKERS

This well-known prayer was composed sometime in the early 20th century and, in the middle of that same century, was attributed to St. Francis of Assisi (1181-1226).

Lord, make me an instrument of your peace.
Where there is hatred, let me sow love;
where there is injury, pardon;
where there is discord, unity;
where there is doubt, faith;
where there is error, truth;
where there is despair, hope;
where there is sadness, joy;
where there is darkness, light.

Divine Master, grant that I may not so much seek
to be consoled as to console;
to be understood as to understand;
to be loved as to love.

For it is in giving that we receive;
it is in pardoning that we are pardoned,
and it is in dying that we are born to eternal life.

COME, HOLY SPIRIT

It has been a tradition, as a private devotion, to ask for the grace of the Holy Spirit. This practice is especially suitable during the Eastertide. To do so, families may use the following prayer.

All: Come, Holy Spirit,
         fill the hearts of your faithful
         and kindle in them the fire of your love.

Leader: Send forth your Spirit, O Lord,

All: and renew the face of the earth.

Leader: O God, on the first Pentecost
         you instructed the hearts of those who believed in you
         by the light of the Holy Spirit:
         under the inspiration of the same Spirit,
         give us a taste for what is right and true
         and a continuing sense
         of his joy-bringing presence and power,
         through Jesus Christ our Lord.

All: Amen.

Soul of Christ

(ANIMA CHRISTI)

The *Anima Christi* is a prayer from around the first half of the 14th century. It is still widely used after receiving the Body and Blood of our Lord Jesus Christ in Holy Communion.

Soul of Christ, make me holy.
Body of Christ, save me.
Blood of Christ, inebriate me.
Water from the side of Christ, wash me clean.
Passion of Christ, strengthen me.
Kind Jesus, hear me.
Hide me within your wounds.
Let me never be separated from you.
Defend me from evil.
In the hour of my death call me to yourself,
that with your saints I may praise you
in everlasting life.

Amen.

Modern Text:

Soul of Christ, sanctify me.
Body of Christ, heal me.
Blood of Christ, drench me.
Water from the side of Christ, wash me.
Passion of Christ, strengthen me.
Good Jesus, hear me.
In your wounds shelter me.
From turning away keep me.
From the evil one protect me.
At the hour of my death call me.
Into your presence lead me,
to praise you with all your saints
for ever and ever.

Amen.

ANGEL OF GOD (Child's Prayer for Protection)

Pious Catholic belief assigns to each person a special angel who watches over the bodily and spiritual health of that person, according to the words of Jesus: "Take care that you do not despise one of these little ones; for, I tell you, in heaven their angels continually see the face of my Father in heaven" (*Matthew* 18.10-11; cf. *Acts* 12.15). In 1670, Pope Clement X (1670-1676) instituted the feast in honor of our personal Guardian Angels, that is today celebrated on October 2.

The Prayer to One's Guardian Angel (sometimes called by its original Latin name, *Angele Dei*) is probably an 11th - 12th century addition to a prayer originally composed by Reginald of Canterbury, who died sometime after 1109.

Angel of God, my guardian dear,
To whom God's love commits me here;
Ever this day, be at my side
To light and guard
To rule and guide.

Traditional

Modern Text:

Angel of God, my guardian dear,
to whom God's love commits me here;
Watch over me throughout the night,
keep me safe within your sight.

WAY OF THE CROSS

The *Way of the Cross*, also called *Stations of the Cross* or, in Latin, *Via Crucis* or *Via Dolorosa*, is one of the most popular pious exercises among the faithful, especially during the season of Lent. Why? Because the events of the Passion and death of Christ have been difficult to understand. His disciples had to read anew everything that was written about him "in the law of Moses, the Prophets, and the Psalms" *(Luke 24, 44)* in order to understand that Jesus had just fulfilled it. On the Cross, Christ's death itself appeared to be "a stumbling block to Jews and foolishness to Gentiles" *(1 Corinthians 1.23)*. That's the reason why the disciples of Jesus remembered and meditated on these events. The fruit of their meditation have been the accounts in two chapters of the Passion written by the four evangelists *(see Matthew 26.1 - 27.66; Mark 14.1 - 15.47; Luke 22.1 - 23.56; John 18.1 - 19.42)* that the Church reads every year on Palm Sunday and on Good Friday. The evangelists remembered how Jesus prophesied his Passion on different occasions *(see Matthew 16.21-23; 17.22-23; 20.17-19 and parallels)* and how he insisted on the commitment of being his followers: "If any want to become my followers, let them deny themselves and take up their cross daily and follow me." *(Luke 9.23)* That's the reason why the faithful draw inspiration from the crucified Christ. He himself has been consistent in teaching the Good News, even in the supreme event of his Passion and death on the Cross.

Along the centuries, the faithful made pilgrimages to Jerusalem with the ideal of walking precisely in the footsteps of their Master. But this was not a common option for many of the faithful because of geographical reasons. Hence the practice of reproducing the Way of the Cross (*Via Crucis*) in different parts of the world where the faithful were living, especially along the walls of their place of worship. A common form is the one divided in 14 Stations, promoted by the Franciscan St. Leonardo of Port-Maurice (1676-1751) and approved by the Apostolic See in the middle of the 17th century.

Recently alternative forms have been introduced. One of these is the addition of a concluding reference to the Resurrection of Jesus – eventually through a 15th station – in order to "complete" the devotion to the Passion. Another is a series of scriptural stations, which begins with the Agony of Jesus in Gethsemane and omits some of the traditional non-scriptural stations in favor of incidents mentioned in the gospels. Pope John Paul II, for example, celebrated a series of scriptural stations on Good Friday in 1991, and again in 1994, in the Colosseum in Rome:

1. Jesus prays in agony in the Garden of Olives;
2. Jesus is arrested when Judas betrays him;
3. Jesus is accused by the Sanhedrin;
4. Jesus is denied by Peter;
5. Jesus is judged by Pilate;
6. Jesus is scourged and crowned with thorns;
7. Jesus carries the Cross;
8. Jesus is helped by Simon of Cyrene;
9. Jesus meets the women of Jerusalem;
10. Jesus is crucified;
11. Jesus promises redemption to the good thief;
12. Jesus speaks to Mary and to John at the foot of the Cross;
13. Jesus dies on the Cross;
14. Jesus is laid in the tomb.

The following is the traditional form.*

SIGN OF THE CROSS

On the last Supper, Jesus, who had repeatedly announced his Passion (cf. *Matthew* 16.21-23; 17.22-23; 20.17-19), said to his disciples: "If they persecuted me, they will persecute you. (...) They will do all these things to you on account of my name, because they do not know him who sent me" (*John* 15.20, 21). In the way of the Cross, as in our Christian journey, we intend to faithfully walk in the steps of Jesus, even at the time of trial.

All make the sign of the cross, as the Leader says:

Leader: In the name of the Father, and of the Son, ✠ and of the Holy Spirit.

All: Amen.

---

* The prayers are adapted from the Way of the Cross done in the city of Toronto on World Youth Day 2002 in Canada. See: *The Way of the Cross in the Heart of the City: Meditations and Prayers, John Paul II* (Novalis: Ottawa, 2003, 2006) 59 pages.

The sung verses, at the end of each station, are taken from the English version (James Quinn, b. 1919) of the medieval Latin hymn *"Stabat Mater Dolorosa"*. See: *CBW III*, 694.

1ˢᵗ Station – Jesus is Condemned to Death

Jesus, the One who will be the glorious Judge of all, at the end of time (cf. *Matthew* 25.31-46), has been judged by human beings and was unjustly condemned.
Indeed he had recommended to his disciples, "Do not judge, so that you may not be judged. (...) You hypocrite, first take the log out of your own eye, and then you will see clearly to take the speck out of your neighbor's eye" (*Matthew* 7.1, 5). In our Christian journey, we are called to be merciful at all times and let the judgment be rendered by God alone.

Leader: We adore you, O Christ, and we praise you.

All genuflect, health permitting.

All: Because by your Holy Cross
          you have redeemed the world.

Scripture Reading

Pilate already said three times to the Jews, "I find no case against him." Now it was the day of Preparation for the Passover; and it was about noon. He said to the Jews, "Here is your King!" They cried out, "Away with him! Away with him! Crucify him!" Pilate asked them, "Shall I crucify your King?" The chief priests answered, "We have no king but Caesar." Then he handed him over to them to be crucified. (cf. *John* 18.38; 19.4, 6, 14-16)

Silence.

Prayer

Our Father....
Hail Mary....
Glory be....

Lord Jesus Christ, you accepted an unjust judgment. Grant to us and to all men and women of our time the grace to remain faithful to the truth. Do not allow the weight of responsibility for the sufferings of the innocent to fall upon us and upon those who come after us. To you, O Jesus, just Judge, be honor and glory for ever and ever. Amen.

Leader: Have mercy on us, O Lord.

All: Have mercy on us.

Verse

When the Stations are performed in public, as in a church or an outdoor procession, it is customary to sing verses or stanzas of "*Stabat Mater*" during the initial prayers, while walking from one Station to the next, and as part of the concluding prayers. See *CBW III*, no. 694.

Jesus on the cross is dying
Soon his body will be lying
In the darkness of the tomb.

2nd Station – JESUS TAKES UP HIS CROSS

When he foretold his death and resurrection, Jesus mentioned to his disciples: "If any want to become my followers, let them deny themselves and take up their cross and follow me." (*Mark* 8.34) In the Way of the Cross, as in our Christian journey, we intend to follow the example of Jesus and to take up our cross.

Leader: We adore you, O Christ, and we praise you.

All genuflect.

All: Because by your Holy Cross
you have redeemed the world.

Scripture Reading

Jesus was handed over to be crucified; and carrying the cross by himself, he was led to what is called The Place of the Skull, which in Hebrew is called "Golgotha". (cf. *John* 19.16-17)

Silence.

Stabat Mater: para. James Quinn, S.J.
Text © James Quinn, S.J., Selah Publishing Co., Inc., North American agent.
www.selahpub.com

Prayer

Our Father....
Hail Mary....
Glory be....

Lord Jesus Christ, you accepted the Cross at the hands of men to make of it the sign of God's saving love for humanity. Grant us and all men and women of our time the grace of faith in this infinite love and of being authentic witnesses to the Redemption. To you, O Jesus, Priest and Victim, be praise and glory for ever. Amen.

Leader: Have mercy on us, O Lord.

All: Have mercy on us.

Verse (See *CBW III*, no. 694)

God's own mother, purest maiden,
Sees the sinless One, sin laden,
Blessed fruit of blessed womb.

3rd Station – JESUS FALLS THE FIRST TIME

A tradition affirmed that Jesus was extremely weak during his passion and fell from weakness more than once, since Jesus was scourged (cf. *John* 19.1-2) and because Simon of Cyrene was pressed into service to carry his Cross. It's said that he fell three times on the Way of the Cross, that is, he truly experienced the suffering in walking to Calvary and carrying his Cross.

Leader: We adore you, O Christ, and we praise you.

All genuflect.

All: Because by your Holy Cross
you have redeemed the world.

Scripture Reading

I, the suffering servant, gave my back to those who struck me, and my cheeks to those who plucked my beard; I did not hide my face from insult and spitting. (cf. *Isaiah* 50.6)

Silence.

Prayer

Our Father....
Hail Mary....
Glory be....

O Christ, you fell under the weight of our faults and rose again for our justification. Help us and all who are weighed down by sin to stand up again and continue the journey. Give us the strength of the Spirit to carry, with you, the cross of our weakness. To you, O Jesus, crushed under the weight of our faults, be our praise and love for ever. Amen.

Leader: Have mercy on us, O Lord.

All: Have mercy on us.

Verse (See *CBW III*, no. 694)

Mary's heart for him is aching
As she sees her Son's heart breaking
So that love may be revealed.

4th Station – JESUS MEETS HIS MOTHER

A tradition affirmed that he even met his mother on his way to Calvary, since he talked to some women of Jerusalem (cf. *Luke* 23.27-31) and because the evangelist John noted that the mother of Jesus stood at the foot of the Cross of her Son (cf. *John* 19.25-27). On her lips were the Scriptural words: "Is it nothing to you, all you who pass by? Look and see if there is any sorrow like my sorrow, which was brought upon me" (*Lamentations* 1.12). In our prayer, we remember all families, all parents worrying for the well-being of their children.

Leader: We adore you, O Christ, and we praise you.

All genuflect.

All: Because by your Holy Cross
you have redeemed the world.

Scripture Reading

When the child Jesus was presented in the Temple of
Jerusalem, Simeon said to his mother Mary, "This child is
destined for the falling and the rising of many in Israel, and to
be a sign that will be opposed so that the inner thoughts of
many will be revealed and a sword will pierce your own soul
too." (cf. *Luke* 2.35)

Silence.

Prayer

Our Father....
Hail Mary....
Glory be....

O Mary, you walked the way of the Cross with your Son, your
mother's heart torn by grief, but mindful always of your *fiat* and
fully confident that He, to whom nothing is impossible, would
be able to fulfill his promises. Implore for us and for
generations to come the grace of surrender to God's love. Help
us, in the face of suffering, rejection and trial, however
prolonged and severe, to never doubt his love. To Jesus, your
Son, be honor and glory for ever and ever. Amen.

Leader: Have mercy on us, O Lord.

All: Have mercy on us.

Verse (See *CBW III*, no. 694)

Now at last her heart is feeling
Sorrow's sword, her Son revealing
Thoughts in many hearts concealed.

5th Station – JESUS IS HELPED BY SIMON OF CYRENE TO CARRY HIS CROSS

In words and deeds, Jesus taught a new commandment, "Just as I have loved you, you also should love one another. By this everyone will know that you are my disciples" (*John* 13.35). In our Christian journey, we are called to carry one another's burdens, and in that way we will keep the law of Christ. (cf. *Galations* 6.2)

Leader: We adore you, O Christ, and we praise you.

All genuflect.

All: Because by your Holy Cross
you have redeemed the world.

Scripture Reading

They compelled a passer-by, who was coming in from the country, to carry the cross of Jesus; it was Simon of Cyrene, the father of Alexander and Rufus. (*Luke* 23.26)

Prayer

Silence.

Our Father....
Hail Mary....
Glory be....

O Christ, you gave to Simon of Cyrene the dignity of carrying your Cross. Welcome us too, under its weight; welcome all men and women and grant to everyone the gift of readiness to serve. Do not permit that we should turn away from those who are crushed by the cross of illness, loneliness, hunger, or injustice. As we carry each other's burdens, help us to become witnesses to the gospel of the Cross and witnesses to you, who live and reign for ever and ever. Amen.

Leader: Have mercy on us, O Lord.

All: Have mercy on us.

Verse (See *CBW III*, no. 694)

How could pity not awaken
for the Son of God, forsaken
In the loneliness of death?

6ᵗʰ Station – JESUS' FACE IS WIPED BY VERONICA

According to a tradition in early apocryphal writings (for example, the *Acts of Pilate*, 2ⁿᵈ century), on the road to Calvary a woman called Veronica (in Greek, Bernice) pushed her way through the soldiers escorting Jesus and with a veil wiped the sweat and blood from his face. It is said that that face remained imprinted on the veil, a faithful reflection, a "true icon" (in Latin, "*vera icona*", that is the origin of her name, *Veronica*) and that she also came to his trial before Pilate to claim his innocence. In our Christian journey, we are invited to recognized in each person the image of God (cf. *Genesis* 1.26-27), the face of Christ (cf. *Matthew* 25.40, 45).

Leader: We adore you, O Christ, and we praise you.

All genuflect.

All: . Because by your Holy Cross
you have redeemed the world.

Scripture Reading

Your face, Lord, do I seek.
Do not hide your face from me. (*Psalm* 27.8-9)

Silence.

Prayer

Our Father....
Hail Mary....
Glory be....

Lord Jesus Christ, you accepted a woman's selfless gesture of love, and in exchange ordained that future generations should remember her by the name of your face. Grant that, through the work of our hands, we may become full collaborators of your work of creation and that we may leave in the world the reflection of your infinite love. To you, O Jesus, splendor of the Father's glory, be praise and glory for ever. Amen.

Leader: Have mercy on us, O Lord.

All: Have mercy on us.

Verse (See *CBW III*, no. 694)

Who would not give consolation
In this Mother's desolation
As he breathes his dying breath?

7th Station – JESUS FALLS THE SECOND TIME

According to tradition, Jesus fell to the ground a second time under the Cross. In the dust of the earth laid the Condemned One; on his lips were the words of the Psalmist, "I am a worm, and not human; scorned by others, and despised by the people" (*Psalms* 22.6). But with great effort he got up again to continue his march, inviting us to do the same, every time we fall in our Christian journey. Falling does not mean the end of the road.

Leader: We adore you, O Christ, and we praise you.

All genuflect.

All: Because by your Holy Cross
you have redeemed the world.

Way of the Cross

Scripture Reading

He, the suffering servant, has borne our infirmities and carried our diseases. (cf. *Isaiah* 53.4)

Silence.

Prayer

Our Father....
Hail Mary....
Glory be....

Lord Jesus Christ, Lamb of God, you fell under the weight of human sin and you got up again in order to take it upon yourself and erase it. Give to us, weak men and women, the strength to carry the cross of daily life and to get up again from our falls, so that we may bring to future generations the Gospel of your saving power. To you, O Jesus, our support when we are weak, be praise and glory for ever. Amen.

Leader: Have mercy on us, O Lord.

All: Have mercy on us.

Verse (See *CBW III*, no. 694)

Mary's heart for him is bleeding;
In his blood, for sinners pleading,
God's new law of love is sealed.

8ᵗʰ Station – JESUS MEETS THE WOMEN OF JERUSALEM

Jesus had wept over Jerusalem, "the city that kills the prophets" (*Matthew* 23.37), foretelling the terrible fate that awaited the city, "When you see Jerusalem surrounded by armies, then know that its desolation has come near. (...) Woe to those who are pregnant and to those who are nursing infants in those days! For there will be great distress on the earth and wrath against this people" (*Luke* 21.20, 23). In the year 70, about 40 years after the event of the death-resurrection of Christ, Jerusalem was destroyed again. In our Christian journey, we are invited to hear the voice of Christ and to open the door to him when he comes. (cf. *Revelation* 3.20)

Leader: We adore you, O Christ, and we praise you.

All genuflect.

All: Because by your Holy Cross
         you have redeemed the world.

Scripture Reading

A great number of the people followed Jesus, and among them
were women who were beating their breasts and wailing for him.
But Jesus turned to them and said, "Daughters of Jerusalem, do
not weep for me, but weep for yourselves and for your children.
For the days are surely coming when they will say, 'Blessed are
the barren, and the wombs that never bore, and the breasts that
never nursed.' Then they will begin to say to the mountains, 'Fall
on us;' and to the hills, 'Cover us.' For if they do this when the
wood is green, what will happen when it is dry?" (Luke 23.27-29)

Silence.

Prayer

Our Father....
Hail Mary....
Glory be....

O Christ, you came into this world to visit all those who await
salvation. Grant that our generation will recognize the time of its
visitation and share in the fruits of your redemption. Do not
permit that there should be weeping for us and for the men and
women of our time because we have rejected our merciful
Father's outstretched hand. To you, O Jesus, born of the Virgin
Daughter of Zion, be honor and praise for ever and ever. Amen.

Leader: Have mercy on us, O Lord.

All: Have mercy on us.

Verse (See *CBW III*, no. 694)

"It is done," she hears him crying
At the moment of his dying:
Death by death has now been healed.

9th Station – JESUS FALLS THE THIRD TIME

According to tradition, Jesus fell a third time beneath his Cross. He struggled, got up and kept going. In our Christian journey, we fail time and time again and, though discouraged, we are tempted to stop trying and to give up. Jesus invites us to hope that, through his help, we really can make the changes in our life.

Leader: We adore you, O Christ, and we praise you.

All genuflect.

All: Because by your Holy Cross
            you have redeemed the world.

Scripture Reading

Jesus said to his disciples, "Come to me, all you that are weary and are carrying heavy burdens, and I will give you rest. Take my yoke upon you, and learn from me; for I am gentle and humble of heart, and you will find rest for your souls."

(cf. *Matthew* 11.28-29)

Silence.

Prayer

Our Father....
Hail Mary....
Glory be....

Lord Jesus Christ, through your humiliation beneath the Cross you revealed to the world the price of its redemption. Grant to men and women the light of faith, so that they may recognize you as the suffering servant of God and man. Give them the courage to follow you on the path that leads to life without end, by way of the Cross and self-emptying. To you, O Jesus, our support when we are weak, be honor and glory for ever. Amen.

Leader: Have mercy on us, O Lord.

All: Have mercy on us.

Verse (See *CBW III*, no. 694)

Let me stand beside you, sharing
Grief for Jesus, my sins bearing
On the cross of Calvary.

10th Station – JESUS IS STRIPPED OF HIS GARMENTS

Jesus was stripped of his cloths: the Innocent Condemned appears in all his human frailty. They offered him gall to drink, but he didn't accept it – he didn't want a sedative, willing to be conscious during his agony, he who had said, "No one takes my life from me, but I lay it down of my own accord." (*John* 10.18) In our Christian journey, we remain conscious of our human frailty and, in moments of trial, we freely unite ourselves to the one sacrifice of Christ.

Leader: We adore you, O Christ, and we praise you.

All genuflect.

All: Because by your Holy Cross
         you have redeemed the world.

Scripture Reading

When they came to a place called Golgotha (which means "Place of a Skull"), they offered Jesus wine to drink, mixed with gall; but when he tasted it, he would not drink it. When they had crucified him, they divided his clothes among themselves by casting lots. (cf. *Matthew* 27.33-35)

Silence.

Way of the Cross

Prayer

Our Father....
Hail Mary....
Glory be....

Lord Jesus, with supreme dedication, you accepted death on the Cross for our salvation. Grant to us and to all the world's people a share in your sacrifice on the Cross, so that what we are and what we do may always be a free and conscious sharing in your work of salvation. To you, O Jesus, Priest and Victim, be honor and glory for ever. Amen.

Leader: Have mercy on us, O Lord.

All: Have mercy on us.

Verse (See *CBW III*, no. 694)

By the cross your vigil keeping,
Let me share your silent weeping,
Pierce my heart with sorrow's sword.

11th Station – Jesus Is Nailed to the Cross

The "King of the Jews" (*Matthew* 2.2; 27.11, 29, 37) who, from the first moments of his life, was laid in a wooden manger, (cf. *Luke* 2.7) spent the last moments of his earthly life hung on a wooden cross (cf. *Luke* 23.33). In our Christian journey, we look at the apparently conquered Crucified Jesus and we keep believing in him, remembering his words, "Just as Moses lifted up the serpent in the wilderness, so must the Son of Man be lifted up, that whoever believes in him may have eternal life. (...) When I am lifted up from the earth, I will draw all people to myself." (*John* 3.14-15; 12.32)

Leader: We adore you, O Christ, and we praise you.

All genuflect.

All: Because by your Holy Cross
        you have redeemed the world.

Scripture Reading

Two criminals were led away to be put to death with Jesus. When they came to the place that is called "The Skull," they crucified Jesus there with the criminals, one on his right and one on his left. Then Jesus said, "Father, forgive them; for they do not know what they are doing." (See Luke 23.32-34)

Silence.

Prayer

Our Father....
Hail Mary....
Glory be....

O Christ lifted high, O Love crucified, fill our hearts with your love, so that we may see in your Cross the sign of our redemption and, drawn by your wounds, we may live and die with you, who live and reign with the Father and the Spirit, now and for ever. Amen.

Leader: Have mercy on us, O Lord.

All: Have mercy on us.

Verse (See CBW III, no. 694)

Let me, though in humble fashion,
share with you the bitter passion
Of the Son you brought to birth.

12th Station – JESUS DIES ON THE CROSS

The crucial moment of Christ's death reminds us of his words, "This is my commandment, that you love one another as I have loved you. No one has greater love than this, to lay down one's life for one's friends" (John 15.12-13). In our Christian journey, we are challenged to lay down our lives for the love of God and of neighbor.

Leader: We adore you, O Christ, and we praise you.

All genuflect.

All: Because by your Holy Cross
         you have redeemed the world.

Scripture Reading

It was now about noon, and darkness came over the whole land until three in the afternoon, while the sun's light failed; and the curtain of the temple was torn in two. Then Jesus, crying with a loud voice, said, "Father, into your hands I commend my spirit." Having said this, he breathed his last. *(Luke 23.44-46)*

Silence.

Prayer

Our Father....
Hail Mary....
Glory be....

Lord Jesus Christ, in the moment of your agony you were not indifferent to humanity's fate, and with your last breath you entrusted to the Father's mercy the men and women of every age, with all their weaknesses and sins. Fill us and generations to come with your Spirit of love, so that our indifference will not render vain in us the fruits of your death. To you, crucified Jesus, the wisdom and the power of God, be honor and glory for ever and ever. Amen.

Leader: Have mercy on us, O Lord.

All: Have mercy on us.

Verse (See *CBW III*, no. 694)

Let me bear the wounds of Jesus,
Drink the precious blood that frees us,
Glory only in his cross.

13th Station – JESUS' BODY IS TAKEN DOWN FROM THE CROSS

Knowing that the mother of Jesus stood at the foot of the Cross (cf. *John* 19.25-27), the Church has preserved along the centuries the sorrowful figure of the "Pietà." Mary, holding the pierced and lifeless body of her Son, remembered the words of Simeon, "This child is destined for the falling and the rising of many in Israel, and to be a sign that will be opposed and a sword will pierce you own soul too." (*Luke* 2.34, 35) In our Christian journey, as we face death with Mary, we keep believing with her in her Son, the Conqueror of death and evil.

Leader: We adore you, O Christ, and we praise you.

All genuflect.

All: Because by your Holy Cross
you have redeemed the world.

SCRIPTURE READING

When evening had come, and since it was the day of Preparation, that is, the day before the Sabbath, Joseph of Arimathea, a respected member of the council, who was also himself waiting expectantly for the kingdom of God, went boldly to Pilate and asked for the body of Jesus. Then Pilate wondered if he were already dead; and summoning the centurion, he asked him whether he had been dead for some time. When he learned from the centurion that he was dead, he granted the body to Joseph. Then Joseph bought a linen cloth, and taking down the body, wrapped it in the linen cloth. (*Mark* 15.42-46)

Silence.

Our Father....
Hail Mary....
Glory be....

Prayer

Holy Mary, Mother of all beloved disciples, implore for us the grace of faith, hope, and charity, so that we, like you, may stand without flinching in faith beneath the Cross until our last breath. To your Son, Jesus, our Savior, with the Father and the Holy Spirit, all honor and glory for ever and ever. Amen.

Leader: Have mercy on us, O Lord.

All: Have mercy on us.

Verse (See *CBW III*, no. 694)

Let the cross be my salvation,
Jesus' death my consolation,
In that hour when I must die.

14ᵗʰ Station – JESUS' BODY IS BURIED IN THE TOMB

The body of Jesus, the new Adam, is buried in a garden (cf. *Genesis* 3.23-24; *John* 19.41), in a new tomb "in which no one had ever been laid." (*John* 19.41) A stone is rolled against the door of the tomb: he will not be able to come out from death on his own. But nothing is impossible with God (cf. *Luke* 1.37) and with Jesus, who had said, "Peace I leave with you; my peace I give to you. (...) Do not let your hearts be troubled, and do not let them be afraid." (*John* 14.27)

Leader: We adore you, O Christ, and we praise you.

All genuflect.

All: Because by your Holy Cross
         you have redeemed the world.

Scripture Reading

Joseph of Arimathea bought a linen cloth, and taking down the body, wrapped it in the linen cloth and laid it in a tomb that had been hewn out of the rock. He then rolled a stone against the door of the tomb. Mary Magdalene and Mary the mother of Joses saw where the body was laid. (*Mark* 15.46-47)

Silence.

Prayer

Our Father....
Hail Mary....
Glory be....

Lord Jesus Christ, by the power of the Holy Spirit, you were drawn by the Father from the darkness of death to the light of a new life in glory. Grant that the sign of the empty tomb may speak to us and to future generations and become a wellspring of living faith, generous love, and unshakeable hope. To you, O Jesus, whose presence, hidden and victorious, fills the history of the world, be honor and glory for ever and ever. Amen.

Leader: Have mercy on us, O Lord.

All: Have mercy on us.

Verse (See *CBW III*, no. 694)

Queen of heaven, by the merit
Of your Son let me inherit
Joy with all the saints on high.

CONCLUSION

No final prayer is required to end the Stations of the Cross, except for the sign of the cross.

Sign of the Cross

In the name of the Father, and of the Son, ✠ and of the Holy Spirit. Amen.

MARIAN PRAYERS

HAIL MARY

The *Hail Mary* (sometimes called the *Angelical salutation* or, from the first words in its Latin form, the *Ave Maria*) is commonly described as consisting of two parts. The first part is biblical; it embodies the words used by the Angel Gabriel in saluting the Blessed Virgin, *Hail (Rejoice), full of grace, the Lord is with you (thee)* (Luke 1.28), and borrows – since the 11ᵗʰ century – the greeting of Elizabeth, *Blessed are you (art thou) among women, and blessed is the fruit of your (thy) womb* (Luke 1.42). The names *Mary* and *Jesus* were universally added to this first part respectively in the XIV and XV century (even before, in some places). The second part of the Hail Mary *(Holy Mary, Mother of God, pray for us sinners, now and at the hour of our death)* is ecclesiastical; it is a petition which was added in the 15ᵗʰ century in Florence, Italy, and was officially stated in the universal Church when Pope Pius V (+1572), in 1568, inserted the whole *Hail Mary* (*Ave Maria*, with both parts) in the *Roman Breviary* (*Breviarium Romanum*), reformed after the Council of Trent (1545-1563).

> Hail, Mary, full of grace,
> the Lord is with you;
> blessed are you among women,
> and blessed is the fruit of your womb, Jesus.
> Holy Mary, mother of God,
> pray for us sinners
> now and at the hour of our death. Amen.

OUR LADY OF GUADALUPE

The following is the opening prayer of the feast of Our Lady of Guadalupe, Patron of the Americas (December 12).

> God of power and mercy,
> you blessed the Americas at Tepeyac
> with the presence of the Virgin Mary of Guadalupe.

May her prayers help us
to accept each other as brothers and sisters.
Set your justice in our hearts
that your peace will reign in the world.

We ask this though our Lord Jesus Christ, your Son,
who lives and reigns with you
in the unity of the Holy Spirit,
one God, for ever and ever. Amen.

SEASONAL ANTIPHONS

DURING ADVENT AND CHRISTMAS

Loving Mother of the Redeemer

This antiphon, known in Latin as *Alma Redemptoris Mater*, has been attributed to Hermanus Contractus (11th century).

Loving mother of the Redeemer,
gate of heaven, star of the sea,
assist your people who have fallen
yet strive to rise again.

To the wonderment of nature you bore your Creator,
yet remained a virgin as before.
You who received Gabriel's joyful greeting,
have pity on us poor sinners.

During Lent and Ordinary Time

We Turn to You for Protection

This antiphon, known in Latin as *Sub tuum Praesidium*, is the oldest known prayer to the Virgin. It was composed in the 3rd century and attested to by an Egyptian papyrus of the 4th century.

Sub tuum præsidium confúgimus,
sancta Die Génetrix;
Nostras deprecatiónes ne despícias
in necessitátibus
sed a perículis cunctis líbera nos semper,
Virgo gloriósa et benedícta.
3rd Century

Modern Translation

We turn to you for protection,
O holy Mother of God.
Listen to our prayers
and help us in our needs.
Save us from every danger,
O glorious and blessed Virgin.

Or:

Queen of Heaven! Queen of Angels!

This antiphon, known in Latin as *Ave, Regina caelorum*, appears to be of monastic origin of the 10th century and the author is unknown. It was traditionally recited from the Feast of the Presentation of the Lord (February 2) until Wednesday in Holy Week.

Queen of heaven! Queen of angels!
Root of Jesse! Gate of morning!
Mother of the world's true light!

Joy to you, glorious virgin,
fairest in heaven where all are fair,
plead with Christ our sins to spare.

Traditional and Common Prayers

During the Easter Season

Queen of Heaven

This antiphon, known in Latin as *Regina Caeli*, appears to have been initially used in Rome as an Antiphon for Vespers at Easter. The author of *Regina Caeli* is unknown, but by virtue of its presence (or absence) in manuscripts, it had to have been composed sometime in the 10th or 11th centuries. One possible author in that time period is Pope Gregory V (d.998). Today the *Regina Caeli* is used as hymn of joy during the Easter Season (Easter Sunday until Pentecost Sunday) when it is used in place of the *Angelus* and prescribed to be recited at Night Prayer (Compline).

Regina cæli, laetáre, allelúia,
quia quem meruísti portáre, allelúia,
resurréxit sicut dixit, allelúia;
ora pro nobis Deum, allelúia.

Modern Translation

Queen of heaven, rejoice, alleluia.
For Christ, your Son and Son of God, alleluia,
has risen as he said, alleluia.
Pray to God for us, alleluia.

During Ordinary Time

Hail, Holy Queen

This antiphon, known in Latin as *Salve Regina*, is said to be the most popular Marian antiphon. Although its author is unknown, the *Chronicles of Spires*, Germany, tell us that the final three invocations, *O clement, O loving, O kind Virgin Mary* (in Latin, *O clemens, O pia, O dulcis Virgo*), were added by St. Bernard (1090-1153).

Salve, Regína, mater misericórdiæ;
vita, dulcédo et spes nostra, salve.
Ad te clamámus, éxsules fílii Evæ.
Ad te suspirámus, geméntes et flentes
in hac lacrimárum valle.

Eia ergo, advocáta nostra,
illos tuos misericórdes óculos
ad nos convérte.
Et Iesum, benedíctum fructum ventris tui,
nobis post hoc exílium osténde.
O clemens, o pia, o dulcis Virgo María.

Traditional Translation.

Hail, holy Queen, mother of mercy,
our life, our sweetness, and our hope.
To you do we cry, poor banished children of Eve.
To you we send up our sighs,
mourning and weeping in this valley of tears.

Turn then, most gracious advocate,
your eyes of mercy upon us,
and after this, our exile,
show unto us the blessed fruit of your womb, Jesus.
O clement, O loving, O kind Virgin Mary.

Modern Translation

Hail, holy Queen, Mother of mercy,
hail, our life, our sweetness, and our hope.
To you we cry, the children of Eve;
to you we send up our sighs,
mourning and weeping in this land of exile.

Turn, then, most gracious advocate,
your eyes of mercy toward us;
lead us home at last
and show us the blessed fruit of your womb, Jesus:
O clement, O loving, O sweet Virgin Mary.

ANGELUS (DURING THE YEAR, OUTSIDE OF EASTER SEASON)

The *Angelus Domini* is a traditional form used to commemorate the holy annunciation of the angel Gabriel to Mary. It is used three times daily: at dawn (6 am), midday (12 noon), and at dusk (6 pm). Traditionally it is recited kneeling while a bell is rung. During the Easter season, the *Angelus Domini* is replaced by the *Regina Caeli*, a practice first instituted on April 2, 1742, by Pope Benedict XIV. Its origins undoubtedly lie with an 11th century custom of reciting three Hail Mary's during the evening bell. Pope Gregory IX (d. 1241) ordered a bell to be rung in the evening to remind people to pray for the Crusades.

Leader: The angel spoke God's message to Mary,

All: and she conceived of the Holy Spirit.

Hail Mary....

Leader: "I am the lowly servant of the Lord:

All: let it be done to me according to your word."

Hail Mary....

Leader: And the Word became flesh

All: and lived among us.

Hail Mary....

Leader: Pray for us, holy Mother of God,

All: that we may become worthy
of the promises of Christ.

Leader: Let us pray.

Lord,
fill our hearts with your grace:
once, through the message of an angel
you revealed to us the incarnation of your Son;
now, through his suffering and death
lead us to the glory of his resurrection.

We ask this though Christ our Lord.

All: Amen.

REGINA CAELI (During the Easter Season when replacing the *Angelus*)

Queen of heaven, rejoice, alleluia.
For Christ, your Son and Son of God, alleluia,
has risen as he said, alleluia.
Pray to God for us, alleluia.

Leader: Rejoice and be glad, O Virgin Mary, alleluia.

All: For the Lord has truly risen, alleluia.

Leader: Let us pray.

God of life,
you have given joy to the world
by the resurrection of your Son,
our Lord Jesus Christ.
Through the prayers of his mother, the Virgin Mary,
bring us to the happiness of eternal life.

We ask this through Christ our Lord.

All: Amen.

REMEMBER, MOST LOVING VIRGIN MARY

The *Memorare* is a 16th century version of a 15th century Latin prayer that began "*Ad sanctitatis tuae pedes, dulcissima Virgo Maria.*" Fr. Claude Bernard (1588-1641) popularized the idea that the *Memorare* was written by Saint Bernard (1090-1153).

Remember, most loving Virgin Mary,
never was it heard
that anyone who turned to you for help
was left unaided.

Inspired by this confidence,
though burdened by my sins,
I run to your protection
for you are my mother.

Mother of the Word of God,
do not despise my words of pleading
but be merciful and hear my prayer. Amen.

THE ROSARY

Rosary means a *crown of roses*, a spiritual bouquet given to the Blessed Mother. The first clear historical reference to the Rosary is from the life of St. Dominic de Guzmán (1170-1221), who founded the Order of Preachers, better known as the Dominicans. He preached a form of the Rosary in France at the time that the Albigensian heresy was devastating the faith there. Tradition has it that the Blessed Mother herself asked for the practice as an antidote for heresy and sin. One of Dominic's future disciples, Alain de Roche (1428 - c.1475-79), began to establish Rosary Confraternities to promote the praying of the Rosary. The form of the Rosary we have today is believed to date from his time. In 1569, St. Pope Pius V, himself a Dominican, issued an apostolic letter establishing the fifteen-Mystery form of the Holy Rosary as the official, Church-authorized version, which was used for the next four centuries. In the year 2002, Pope John Paul II published an apostolic letter that added five more Mysteries (*Luminous Mysteries*).

The Rosary is sometimes called the Dominican Rosary, to distinguish it from other rosary-like prayers (e.g. Franciscan Rosary of the Seven Joys, Servite Rosary of the Seven Sorrows). It is also, in a general sense, a form of chaplet or *corona* (also referring to a crown), of which there are many varieties in the Church. Finally, in English it has been called "Our Lady's Psalter" or "the beads." This last derives from an Old English word for prayers (bede) and to request (biddan or bid).

"As a prayer for peace, the Rosary is also, and always has been, *a prayer of and for the family*. At one time this prayer was particularly dear to Christian families, and it certainly brought them closer together. It is important not to lose this precious inheritance. We need to return to the practice of family prayer and prayer for families, continuing to use the Rosary." (John Paul II, Apostolic Letter *Rosarium Virginis Mariae* [October 16, 2002] n. 41).

While praying the Rosary, the Church encourages us to meditate on God's plan for saving the world by sending his Son as our Savior. This is done by reflecting on the "mysteries" or events of the life of the Lord Jesus.

Joyful Mysteries (Monday and Saturdays)

- Annunciation of our Lord.
  See *Luke* 1.26-38, John 1.1-14, *Hebrews* 1.1-4

- Visitation.
  See *Luke* 1.39-56

- Birth of our Lord.
  See *Luke* 2.1-20, *Matthew* 2.1-14, *Galatians* 4.4-7

- Jesus is presented in the temple.
  See *Luke* 2.22-38

- Jesus is found in the temple.
  See *Luke* 2.41-52

Sorrowful Mysteries (Tuesdays and Friday)

- Agony of Jesus in the garden.
  See *Matthew* 26.36-56, *Mark* 14.32-52, *Luke* 22.39-53, *John* 18.1-11

- Jesus is scourged.
  See *Matthew* 27.20-26, *Mark* 15.6-15, *Luke* 23.13-25, *John* 18.38-19.1

- Jesus is crowned with thorns.
  See *Matthew* 27.27-30, *Mark* 15.16-20, *John* 19.2-7

- Jesus carries his cross.
  See *Matthew* 27.31-33, *Mark* 15.20-22, *Luke* 23.26-32, *John* 19.17

- Jesus is crucified.
  See *Matthew* 27.34-56, *Mark* 15.23-41, *Luke* 23.33-49, *John* 19.18-37

Glorious Mysteries (Wednesday and Sunday)

- Jesus is raised from the dead.
  See *Matthew* 28.1-10, *Mark* 16.1-18, *Luke* 24.1-12, *John* 20.1-10

- Jesus ascends into heaven.
  See *Mark* 16.19-20, *Luke* 24.50-53, *Acts* 1.9-11

- Jesus sends his Spirit upon the Church.
  See *John* 16.4-15, *Acts* 2.1-12

- Mary is assumed into heaven.
  See *1 Corinthians* 15.20-26 or 15.54-57, *Revelation* 12.1-5

- Mary is crowned queen of heaven.
  See *Luke* 1.46-55

Luminous Mysteries (Thursday)

- Jesus is baptized in the Jordan.
  See *Matthew* 3.13-14, *Mark* 1.9-11, *Luke* 3.21-22, *John* 1.29-34

- The Manifestation at Cana.
  See *John* 2.1-12

- Jesus proclaims the Reign of God (...and calls to Conversion).
  See *Matthew* 4.12-17, *Mark* 1.14-15, *Luke* 4.14-15
  also *Matthew* 9.2-8, *Mark* 3.3-13, *Luke* 7.47-48, *John* 20.22-23

- Jesus is transfigured.
  See *Matthew* 17.1-8, *Mark* 9.2-8, *Luke* 9.28-36, *1 Peter* 1.16-18

- The Institution of the Eucharist.
  See *Matthew* 26.26-29, *Mark* 14.22-26, *Luke* 22.14-23,
  John 13.1-17, *1 Corinthians* 11.23-26

MARIAN LITANIES

"Litanies are to be found among the prayers to the Blessed Virgin recommended by the Magisterium. These consist in a long series of invocations of Our Lady, which follow in a uniform rhythm, thereby creating a stream of prayer characterized by insistent praise and supplication. The invocations, generally very short, have two parts: the first of praise (*Virgo clemens*), the other of supplication (*Ora pro nobis*).

Following the prescription of Leo XIII that the recitation of the Rosary should be concluded by the Litany of Loreto during the month of October, the false impression has arisen among some of the faithful that the Litany is in some way an appendix to the Rosary. The Litanies are independent acts of worship. They are important acts of homage to the Blessed Virgin Mary, or as processional elements, or form part of a celebration of the Word of God or of other acts of worship." (*Directory on popular piety and the Liturgy*, n. 203)

Litany of Loreto

The so called *Litany of Loreto* has its origin in a manuscript of the end of the XII century, today preserved in Paris (Nat. lat. 5267). It was used in the shrine of Loreto at least from the first half of the 16th century, was spread, and became famous.

Leader:	All:
Lord, have mercy.	Lord, have mercy.
Christ, have mercy.	Christ, have mercy.
Lord, have mercy.	Lord, have mercy.
Christ, hear us.	Christ, hear us.
Christ, graciously hear us.	Christ, graciously hear us.
God, the Father of heaven,	have mercy on us.
God the Son, Redeemer of the world,	have mercy on us.
God the Holy Spirit, the Paraclete,	have mercy on us.
Holy Trinity, One God,	have mercy on us.
Holy Mary,	pray for us.
Holy Mother of God,	
Holy Virgin of virgins,	
Mother of Christ,	pray for us.
Mother of the Church,	
Mother of divine grace,	
Mother most pure,	
Mother most chaste,	
Mother ever virgin,	
Immaculate mother,	
Mother worthy of love,	
Mother most admirable,	
Mother of good counsel,	
Mother of the Creator,	
Mother of the Savior,	
Prudent Virgin,	pray for us.
Virgin worthy of honor,	
Virgin worthy of praise,	
Powerful Virgin,	
Clement Virgin,	
Faithful Virgin,	

Mirror of perfection,	pray for us.
Seat of wisdom,	
Source of joy,	
Temple of the Holy Spirit,	
Tabernacle of eternal glory,	
Dwelling consecrated to God,	
Mystical rose,	
Tower of the holy city of David,	
Impregnable fortress,	
Sanctuary of divine presence,	
Ark of the covenant,	
Gate of heaven,	
Morning star,	

Health of the sick,	pray for us.
Refuge of sinners,	
Comforter of the afflicted,	
Help of Christians,	

Queen of angels,	pray for us.
Queen of patriarchs,	
Queen of prophets,	
Queen of the apostles,	
Queen of martyrs,	
Queen of confessors,	
Queen of virgins,	
Queen of all saints,	
Queen conceived without sin,	
Queen assumed into heaven,	
Queen of the rosary,	
Queen of peace,	

Lamb of God, you take away the sins of the world,	forgive us, Lord.
Lamb of God, you take away the sins of the world,	hear us, Lord.
Lamb of God, you take away the sins of the world,	have mercy on us.

V. Pray for us, holy Mother of God.
R. Make us worthy of the promises of Christ.

During Advent

Leader: Let us pray.

God our Father,
in the angel's message,
you willed that the Word
become incarnate in the virginal womb of Mary;
grant your people,
which honors her as true Mother of God,
to always enjoy her maternal intercession.

(We make our prayer) through Christ our Lord.

All: Amen.

During Christmas

Leader: Let us pray.

God our Father,
in the fruitful virginity of Mary,
you have given to humanity
the blessing of eternal salvation;
grant that we may experience her intercession,
since, through her,
we have received the Author of life,
Christ, your Son,
who lives and reigns for ever and ever.

All: Amen.

During Lent

Leader: Let us pray.

God our Father,
when Jesus, your Son, was raised up on the Cross,
it was your will that Mary, his Mother,
    should stand there
and suffer with him in her heart.
Grant that, in union with her,
your holy Church may share in the passion of Christ,
and so be brought to the glory of his resurrection.
Who lives and reigns for ever and ever.

All: Amen.

During Easter

Leader: Let us pray.

God our Father,
in the glorious resurrection of your Son,
you have again given joy to the whole world;
grant that, through the intercession of the Virgin Mary,
we may share the endless joy of eternal life.
(We make our prayer) through Christ our Lord.

All: Amen.

During Ordinary Time

Leader: Let us pray.

Grant to your faithful, Lord, our God,
that we may always enjoy health of body and spirit
and, through the glorious intercession of holy Mary,
ever virgin,
save us from evils which sadden us now,
and guide us to endless joy.
(We make our prayer) through Christ our Lord.

All: Amen.

Biblical Litany to Saint Mary

Along the centuries, the Church referred to the Holy Scripture to address its praise to the blessed Virgin Mary. The following form is divided in two parts which correspond to the Old and New Testaments from which the Marian titles come.

Leader: All:

Lord, have mercy.   Lord, have mercy.
Christ, have mercy.   Christ, have mercy.
Lord, have mercy.   Lord, have mercy.

Christ, hear us.   Christ, hear us.
Christ, graciously hear us.   Christ, graciously hear us.

God the Father of heaven,   have mercy on us.
God the Son, Redeemer of the world,   have mercy on us.
God the Holy Spirit, the Paraclete,   have mercy on us.
Holy Trinity, One God,   have mercy on us.

Holy Mary, Mother of God,   pray for us.

New Eve,   pray for us.
Mother of the living,
Descendant of Abraham,
Heiress of the promise,
Shoot of Jesse,
Daughter of Sion,

Virgin soil,   pray for us.
Ladder of Jacob,
Burning bush,
Tabernacle of the Most High,
Ark of the covenant,
Seat of the wisdom,
City of God,
Gate to the East,
Source of living water,
Dawn of salvation,

Joy of Israel,   pray for us.
Glory of Jerusalem,
Honor of our people,

Virgin of Nazareth,	pray for us.
Virgin full of grace,	
Virgin overshadowed by the Spirit,	
Virgin giving birth,	
Handmaid of the Lord,	pray for us.
Handmaid of the Word,	
Humble and poor handmaid,	
Wife of Joseph,	
Blessed among women,	
Mother of Jesus,	pray for us.
Mother of Emmanuel,	
Mother of the Son of David,	
Mother of the Lord,	
Mother of the disciples,	
Eager mother in the Visitation,	pray for us.
Joyful mother at Bethlehem,	
Generous mother in the Temple,	
Exiled mother in Egypt,	
Anxious mother in Jerusalem,	
Provident mother at Cana,	
Resolute mother on Calvary,	
Prayerful mother in the Cenacle,	
Woman of the new Covenant,	pray for us.
Woman adorned with the sun,	
Woman crowned with stars,	
Queen at the right hand of the King,	pray for us.
Blessed are you	
who believed,	we praise you.
Blessed are you	
who stored up the Word,	we bless you.
Blessed are you	
who did the will of the Father,	we praise you for your glory.

Leader: Let us pray.

God our Father, from one generation to the next,
you revealed your love for humanity:
we give you thanks because,
when the appointed time came,
through the blessed Virgin Mary,
you gave us Jesus, your Son and our Savior;
grant us, we pray, the Spirit of truth
in order to discern in the events of history
the signs of hope and peace,
to gather from the ups and downs of life
the seeds of freedom and grace.
(We make our prayer) through Christ our Lord.

All: Amen.

Litany of Saint Mary of Hope

The *Litany of Saint Mary of Hope* is based on the Marian texts of the Document of Puebla, Mexico, of the third Latin American Bishops' general Conference (January 27 – February 13, 1979). It was first sung in Italian at the Congress of the Italian Church celebrated at Loreto in April 1985. It was then sung in the presence of Pope John Paul II in the Basilica St. Peter on October 3, 1987, at a vigil Prayer for the VII Synod of Bishops on the topic *The Vocation and Mission of the Lay Faithful in the Church and in the World Twenty Years after the Second Vatican Council.*

Leader:	All:
Lord, have mercy.	Lord, have mercy.
Christ, have mercy.	Christ, have mercy.
Lord, have mercy.	Lord, have mercy.
Christ, hear us.	Christ, hear us.
Christ, graciously hear us.	Christ, graciously hear us.
God, the Father of heaven,	have mercy on us.
God the Son, Redeemer of the world,	have mercy on us.
God the Holy Spirit, the Paraclete,	have mercy on us.
Holy Trinity, One God,	have mercy on us.
Holy Mary of hope,	pray for us.
Holy Mary of the way,	
Holy Mary of the light,	
Fullness of Israel,	pray for us.
Prophecy of the new times,	
Dawn of the new world,	
Mother of God,	pray for us.
Mother of the Messiah redeemer,	
Mother of the redeemed,	
Mother of all people,	

R. Holy Mary of hope, enlighten our way.

Virgin of silence,	pray for us.
Virgin of hearing,	
Virgin of singing,	

Handmaid of the Lord,   pray for us.
Handmaid of the Word,
Handmaid of redemption,
Handmaid of the Kingdom,

R. Holy Mary of hope, enlighten our way.

Disciple of Christ,   pray for us.
Witness of the Gospel,
Sister of men and women,

Beginning of the Church,   pray for us.
Mother of the Church,
Model of the Church,
Image of the Church,

R. Holy Mary of hope, enlighten our way.

Mary, blessed among women,   pray for us.
Mary, dignity of women,
Mary, greatness of women,

Faithful woman in expectation,   pray for us.
Faithful woman of commitment,
Faithful woman in discipleship,
Faithful woman at the foot of the cross,

R. Holy Mary of hope, enlighten our way.

First fruit of Easter,   pray for us.
Splendor of Pentecost,
Star of evangelization,

Shining presence,   pray for us.
Prayerful presence,
Welcoming presence,
Active presence,

R. Holy Mary of hope, enlighten our way.

Hope of the poor,   pray for us.
Confidence of the humble,
Support of the marginalized,

Relief of the oppressed,   pray for us.
Defense of the innocent,
Courage of the persecuted,
Comfort of the exiled,

R. Holy Mary of hope, enlighten our way.

Voice of freedom,   pray for us.
Voice of communion,
Voice of peace,

Sign of the maternal face of God,   pray for us.
Sign of the nearness of the Father,
Sign of the mercy of the Son,
Sign of the fruitfulness of the Spirit,

R. Holy Mary of hope, enlighten our way.

Holy Mary of Guadalupe,   pray for us.
Mother of Latin America,
Queen of the Americas,

Christ, Lord of history,   have mercy on us.
Christ, Savior of humanity,
Christ, hope of creation,

Leader: Let us pray.

God our holy Father,
in the journey of the Church,
you have put the blessed Virgin Mary as a bright sign;
through her intercession, sustain our faith
and revive our hope,
so that, led by love,
we may walk with courage in the way of the Gospel.
(We make our prayer) through Christ our Lord.

All: Amen.

PRAYERS TO ST. JOSEPH

PRAYER TO ST. JOSEPH

The four main sections of this prayer underline four titles given to St. Joseph, in history: 1) In the beginning of our Christian era, Joseph became the husband of the Blessed Virgin Mary [feast: March 19]; 2) Over the years, Joseph has become the patron saint of many countries, including Canada, Poland, Italy, Mexico and others. He is also patron of the Americas; 3) On December 8, 1870, he was declared "Patron of the universal Church" by Pope Pius IX; 4) On May 1, 1955, he was proposed by Pope Pius XII as a Model to Workers through the introduction of a feast, *St. Joseph the Worker*, on May 1, Labor Day in many countries.

[Husband of the Blessed Virgin Mary]

Saint Joseph, Illustrious Descendant of David,
Husband of the Mother of God,
Foster-father of the Son of God,
in dream you received from the Almighty
the task of taking Mary as your wife
and Jesus as your Son, conceived from the Holy Spirit,
and of caring for them in the difficult beginnings
   of the New Covenant.
Intercede for us so that your example may remind us
to care for the presence of Jesus and Mary in our lives,
in the trials of today's world.

Zealous guardian of the Redeemer,
Patron of the Church in the Americas,
you were invoked by the first missionaries in the New World
to assist the growth of the seed of Christian faith
courageously sown in these lands.
Intercede for all inhabitants of our hemisphere
who, along the history,
often adopted your name from Baptism
so that all families
may give a central place to your Son in their lives
and in abundance produce the fruits of the Gospel:
love, understanding, forgiveness,
care for one another, holiness and happiness.

[Patron of the universal Church]

Splendor of Patriarchs,
Head of the Holy Family,
you were asked by the Successor of Peter
to watch over the universal Church,
the Family of those who believe in your Son.
Intercede for all Christians
so that they may, at all times,
deny themselves,
take up their cross
and faithfully walk in the footsteps of their Master,
loving God and their neighbor.

Silent and well-known Carpenter in Nazareth,
Model of workers,
by the work of your hands,
you gave your contribution to the work of the Creator,
you earned your living
and you provided for the needs of the Holy Family.
Intercede for all workers, in the difficulties of their daily lives,
especially for the unemployed, in their anxieties for tomorrow,
so that, through the guidance of God,
the great Architect and Builder,
they all may use their strength and their talents
to make visible his Kingdom, his new Creation,
to offer a concrete service to society
and to earn wages worthy of their efforts.

[A holy companion in our Christian journey]

Saint Joseph,
Man of enlightening dreams
Obedient servant of God,
accompany us, with your wife, the Blessed Virgin Mary,
throughout our life
to the glory and praise of God,
now and for ever and ever.
Amen.

LITANY TO ST. JOSEPH

Leader:	All:
Lord, have mercy.	Lord, have mercy.
Christ, have mercy.	Christ, have mercy.
Lord, have mercy.	Lord, have mercy.
Christ, hear us.	Christ, hear us.
Christ, graciously hear us.	Christ, graciously hear us.
God, the Father of heaven,	have mercy on us.
God the Son, Redeemer of the world,	have mercy on us.
God the Holy Spirit, the Paraclete,	have mercy on us.
Holy Trinity, One God,	have mercy on us.
Holy Mary,	pray for us.
Saint Joseph,	pray for us.
Son of Adam,	
Son of Abraham,	
Son of David,	
Righteous man,	pray for us.
Indigent man,	
Patient man,	
Man of unflinching faith,	pray for us.
Man of enlightening dreams,	
Man of prudent silence,	
Discreet servant,	pray for us.
Obedient servant,	
Troubled servant,	
Husband of Mary,	pray for us.
Vigilant husband,	
Faithful husband,	
Well-advised father,	pray for us.
Caring father,	
Courageous father,	

Guardian of your adopted Son,   pray for us.
Guardian of the Holy Family,
Guardian of our Redeemer,

Witness of the joyous birth of Jesus,   pray for us.
Witness of the praising of Simeon and Anna,
Witness of the wondering of the teachers,

Companion of the exiled,   pray for us.
Sustainer of the families,
Model of workers,

Consoler of the afflicted,   pray for us.
Hope of the sick,
Comforter of the dying,

Well-known Carpenter in Nazareth,   pray for us.
Protector of the Church in the Americas,
Patron of the universal Church,

Lamb of God,
you take away the sins of the world,   forgive us, Lord.
Lamb of God,
you take away the sins of the world,   hear us, Lord.
Lamb of God,
you take away the sins of the world,   have mercy on us.

Leader: Pray for us, O holy husband of the Mother of God.

All: That we may be made worthy of the promises of Christ.

Or:

Leader: God made him the master of his household.

All: He gave him charge over all his possessions. (cf. Ps 105.21)

Leader: Let us pray.

Father, in your loving providence you entrusted our
Savior to the care of St. Joseph. By the help of his
prayers may your Church continue to serve its Lord,
Jesus Christ, who lives and reigns with you and the
Holy Spirit, one God, for ever and ever. Amen.

PRAYER TO ST. ANNE AND ST. JOACHIM

"The tree is known by its fruit" (*Matthew* 12.33; 7.16, 20), said Jesus. We know Christ, the flower and sweet fruit that came from the branch, the Blessed Virgin Mary, who was kept sinless by God from the first moment of her conception. From the holiness of the fruit, we may say that the tree, her parents, was holy. According to the apocryphal *Protogospel of James* (2nd century), the parents of the Blessed Virgin Mary were called Anne (also spelled *Ann, Anne, Anna*, from Hebrew, *Hannah*, that is, grace) and Joachim (that is, *the Lord prepares*). The veneration of the grandparents of Jesus is very old in the East, where on a July 25 in about 550, a basilica in Constantinople was dedicated to St. Anne. In the West such veneration appeared only in the 8th century. In 1584, the names of St. Anne and St. Joachim were inserted by Pope Gregory XIII in the Roman Liturgical Calendar.

Devotion to St. Anne was brought to the Americas by the early colonists from Brittany (France) and adopted quickly by the native communities. In their culture the peoples of the First Nations have great respect for their ancestors who venerated St. Anne, the grandmother of Jesus. The shrine of St. Anne de Beaupré, established in 1658 and raised to the rank of a minor basilica on May 5, 1887, is a famous place of pilgrimage for both Canadians and Americans, as is Lac Ste Anne in Alberta since June 1889.

St. Anne and St. Joachim,
you were especially favored by God,
on the threshold of the New Testament,
to be the parents of the Blessed Virgin Mary, Mother of God.
You provided your daughter
with a loving home, family and faithful teaching,
and brought her up
to be the worthy Mother of our Savior, Jesus Christ.
Your way of parenting was for her an example
to bring forth the only-begotten Son of God, Jesus,
treasuring all things in her heart. (cf. *Lk* 2.19, 51)
Your faith laid the foundation of courage and strength
that allowed Mary to stand by the Cross as her Son was crucified
and to still believe. (cf. *Jn* 19.25-27)
In communion with Mary and Joseph,
intercede to your grandson Jesus for all parents,
so that they may help their children,
to grow in strength and in knowledge
and to discover the mission that God entrusts to them
in the world and in the Church.

Good St. Anne,
Mother of Mary, the Blessed one among women, (cf. *Luke* 1.42)
you were thanked by the newcomers on this glorious and free land
for your protecting intercession
     during their uncertain voyage across the ocean.
and you were invoked by them
in their trials in establishing new homes and traditions.
Intercede for all our families
so that, through the help of the Holy Spirit,
we may grow together in peace and understanding
and make our home hospitable to our visitors and guests.
May we persevere, like you, in the love of Jesus and Mary
and live pure and blameless lives in the sight of God.

Grandmother of Jesus, our Savior,
you were honored by the First Nations people of this land
in your role of nurturing him and bringing him up to maturity.
Intercede for all grandmothers,
so that they may nurture their grandchildren
     with love and wisdom,
teaching them to find their way in life
and to be right in word and in deed.

Gentle St. Joachim,
Father of the Virgin Handmaid of the Lord, (cf. *Luke* 1.38)
Grandfather of Jesus,
among your descendants, you had the privilege
to count the One whom your own ancestors longed to see,
the long expected Messiah.
Intercede for all elders and grandfathers,
who worked hard on this land, defending its integrity,
and who grew old in the service of the Almighty.
May God grant them
to benefit from their remaining strength,
to share the wealth of their experience and wisdom
and to enter his Kingdom at the end of their earthly time.

Good St. Anne and St. Joachim,
Parents of Mary, the "favored one," (*Luke* 1.28)
accompany us, in our faith journey on this land,
to the glory and praise of God,
now and for ever and ever. Amen.

LITANY OF THE SAINTS
(PROPER TO THE UNITED STATES)

The names of saints which have local significance may be added in the proper place in the litany. These might include, the patron saint, the titular of the church, the founder of an institute or congregation. Petitions adapted to the place or circumstances may be added to the petitions for various needs. For convenience, the categories of the saints and petitions are indicated in square brackets.

I. Supplication to God

Leader:

Lord, have mercy.
Christ, have mercy.
Lord, have mercy.

All:

Lord, have mercy.
Christ, have mercy.
Lord, have mercy.

II. Invocation of the Saints

[Mary and the Angels]

Holy Mary, Mother of God,   pray for us.
Saint Michael,
Holy angels of God,

[Prophets and Precursors of the Faith]

Abraham, Moses, and Elijah,   pray for us.
Saint Joachim and Saint Anne,
Saint Joseph,
Saint John the Baptist,

[Apostles and Followers of Christ]

Saint Peter and Saint Paul,   pray for us.
Saint Andrew,
Saint John,
Saint Mary Magdalene,

Saint Stephen,   pray for us.
Saint Ignatius,
Saint Lawrence,
Saint Perpetua and Saint Felicity,
Saint Agnes,
Saint Isaac Jogues and Saint René Goupil,

[Bishops and Doctors]

Saint Gregory,   pray for us.
Saint Augustine,
Saint Athanasius,
Saint Basil,
Saint Catherine of Sienna,
Saint Teresa of Avila,
Saint Martin,
Saint John Neumann,

[Priests and Religious]

Saint Benedict,   pray for us.
Saint Francis and Saint Dominic,
Saint Francis Xavier,
Saint John Vianney,
Saint Elizabeth Ann Seton,
Saint Rose Philippine Duchesne,
Saint Mother Théodore Guérin,
Saint Frances Xavier Cabrini,
Saint Katharine Drexel

[Laity]

Saint Monica,   pray for us.
Saint Louis,
Blessed Kateri Tekakwitha,
All holy men and women,

III. Invocations to Christ

[General Invocations, always used]

Lord, be merciful,	Lord, save us.
From all harm,	Lord, save us.
From every sin,	Lord, save us.
From all temptations,	Lord, save us.
From everlasting death,	Lord, save us.
By your coming among us,	Lord, save us.
By your death and rising to new life,	Lord, save us.
By your gift of the Holy Spirit,	Lord, save us.
Be merciful to us sinners,	Lord, hear our prayer.

[General Petitions, always used, except at the Easter Vigil]

Guide and protect your holy Church,	Lord, hear our prayer.
Keep our pope and all clergy in faithful service to your Church,	Lord, hear our prayer.
Bring all peoples together in trust and peace,	Lord, hear our prayer.
Strengthen us in your service,	Lord, hear our prayer.

IV. Petitions

Bless the fruits of the earth and all human labor,	Lord, hear our prayer.
Deliver us from disease, hunger and war,	Lord, hear our prayer.
Bring all Christians together in unity,	Lord, hear our prayer.
Grant eternal rest to all who have died in the faith,	Lord, hear our prayer.

V. Conclusion

Jesus, Son of the living God.	Lord, hear our prayer.
Christ, hear us.	Christ, hear us.
Lord Jesus, hear our prayer.	Lord Jesus, hear our prayer.

The Litany of the Saints may be concluded by this prayer, unless there is a more suitable one for a specific celebration.

Leader: Let us pray.

God, source of all holiness,
your have enriched your Church
with many gifts in the Saints.
Direct, O Lord, our actions by your holy inspirations,
and carry them on by your gracious assistance,
that every prayer and work of ours
may always begin with you,
and through you be happily ended.

Grant this through Christ our Lord.

All: Amen.

Interceding

FOR ALL PEOPLE

God's people are called to pray for all people and for all the needs of the universe, in order that God's kingdom may come among us. As God's people of prayer, we show our concern for others and for their needs, including their salvation.

Some of these intercessions may be included at any time of prayer.

Leader: For all the people living in this world.
For the people of God in the Church on earth.
For our pope and for the bishops of the world.
For our bishop.
For the priests, deacons and religious of our diocese.
For the people of our civil community and our parish.

For those who govern or lead or teach us.
For all who suffer in disaster or war.
For those who are crushed by injustice
   or other burdens.
For young and old, parents and children.
For the sick and the dying.
For young people preparing for marriage.
For those who have asked us to pray for them.
For other persons.
For those who have died.

For peace and harmony among nations.
For suitable weather and good crops.
For an increase of vocations.
For unity among all Christians.
For the conversion of sinners.
For our personal needs.

After a few moments of silence, we may conclude our general prayer in these words.

Leader: Blessed are you, Lord,
maker of heaven and earth:
you have shown us your love
by calling us to be your beloved sons and daughters
and members of your holy people, your Church.

Listen to the prayers we offer to you,
and in your love for us, grant what we ask in faith.

We give you glory and praise, eternal Father,
through Jesus your Son,
in the unity of your Spirit,
one God, for ever and ever.

All: Amen.

Or:

Leader: Lord God,
listen to these and all our needs.
Grant what we ask in faith,
through Christ our Lord.

All: Amen.

FOR THIS COMMUNITY

These intercessions may be included in any celebration and adapted to local need. The response may be sung. The concluding prayer may be taken from any of the prayers for particular needs. Another minister may read the intercessions, with the leader reciting the opening and concluding prayers.

Leader: Let us pray in silence
for the needs of this community.

All pause for a moment of silent prayer.

For all the people of our community,
we pray to the Lord.

All: R. Lord, have mercy.

Leader: For peace and harmony,
we pray to the Lord. R.

For our families and friends,
we pray to the Lord. R.

For our civic and religious leaders,
we pray to the Lord. R.

For all who work for the good of others,
we pray to the Lord. R.

For all who suffer pain, loss and sorrow,
we pray to the Lord. R.

For all who believe in God,
we pray to the Lord. R.

Other intentions may be added.

Leader: In our times of work and recreation,
we pray to the Lord. R.

In all seasons, by day and by night,
we pray to the Lord. R.

Leader: Lord,
listen to our prayers
for the men, women and children of our community.
Bless us and guide all our actions.
Be with us at all times,
for we place our lives in your hands
now and for ever.

All: Amen.

A seasonal prayer may also be used as the conclusion.

SOLEMN INTERCESSIONS

These intercessions may be used at times of special prayer, including days of reflection and retreat. These prayers may be adapted, and further petitions added. The response may be sung.

The leader invites all to join in prayer:

Leader: Let us pray to God our Father
for his beloved Church and for all humanity.

For each petition, a reader or other minister reads the intention, all pause for silent prayer, the minister says the prayer, and all respond.

The leader concludes the intercessions with the final prayer.

Leader: We pray for the Church of God:

All pause for a moment of silent prayer.

Bless your beloved people,
and fill us with your love,
so that we may do your will each day.
Hear us, O Lord.

All: Lord, save your people.

Leader: We pray for the pope
and for the bishops of the world.

All pause for a moment of silent prayer.

Guide Pope *N.* and our spiritual leaders,
and help them to teach the truth of Christ to all.
Hear us, O Lord.

All: Lord, save your people.

Leader: We pray for our Bishop *N.*
and for the priests, deacons,
and religious of our diocese.

All pause for a moment of silent prayer.

Bless your ministers in their work for your glory
and guide them by your Spirit.
Hear us, O Lord.

All: Lord, save your people.

Leader: We pray for the family of our (St. *N.'s*) parish:

All pause for a moment of silent prayer.

Bless our parents and children, the youth and the aged,
and bless every home in our parish community.
Hear us, O Lord.

All: Lord, save your people.

Leader: We pray for all the people of this world:

All pause for a moment of silent prayer.

Grant peace and justice to all nations,
and guide those who govern them,
so that men and women around the world
will follow Christ in love.
Hear us, O Lord.

All: Lord, save your people.

Leader: We pray for good weather and good crops:

All pause for a moment of silent prayer.

Smile upon our land and grant us plentiful harvests,
so that we may share our food and wealth
with the poor and needy and starving of the world.
Hear us, O Lord.

All: Lord, save your people.

Leader: We pray for those who are suffering
in disasters or war:

All pause for a moment of silent prayer.

Look with compassion on people who suffer disaster,
or whose lands are ravaged by war and hatred.
Open the hearts of your people to help those in need.
Hear us, O Lord.

All: Lord, save your people.

Leader: We pray for the sick and the dying:

All pause for a moment of silent prayer.

Have mercy on the sick and the dying,
and teach them to accept their cross with Jesus.
Make us more understanding
and kind toward all who suffer.
Hear us, O Lord.

All: Lord, save your people.

Leader: We pray for more vocations
among the young of this parish:

All pause for a moment of silent prayer.

Make our youth and their parents more generous,
so that more young men and women
may answer your call
and devote their lives to serving your people.
Hear us, O Lord.

All: Lord, save your people.

Leader: We pray for all those preparing for marriage:

All pause for a moment of silent prayer.

Help those who are preparing to marry in Christ.
Grant them pure love and a spirit of generous prayer.
Bless their marriage and their families,
and lead them always in your peace and love.
Hear us, O Lord.

All: Lord, save your people.

Leader: We pray for unity among all Christians.

All pause for a moment of silent prayer.

Let your Spirit bring your people together,
so that all who believe in your Son
may be one in their faith and love.
Hear us, O Lord.

All: Lord, save your people.

Leader: We pray for conversion of heart among your people:

All pause for a moment of silent prayer.

Stir up the hearts of your people
to turn away from sin
and come back to you in prayer,
repentance, and love.
Hear us, O Lord.

All: Lord, save your people. ➤

The leader concludes with these or similar words.

Leader: Blessed are you, eternal Father,
maker of heaven and earth:
you have shown us your love
by calling us to be your beloved sons and daughters
and members of your holy people, your Church.

Listen to the prayers we offer to you,
and in your love for us, grant what we ask in faith.

We give you glory and praise, eternal Father,
through Jesus your Son,
in the unity of your Spirit,
one God, for ever and ever.

All: Amen.

A seasonal prayer may also be used as the conclusion.

Index

Blessings and Prayers

Blessings and Prayers